Accumula 1

STUDENT BOOK

JUMP Math
One Yonge Street, Suite 1014
Toronto, Ontario M5E 1E5
Canada
www.jumpmath.org

Writers: Dr. John Mighton, Dr. Sohrab Rahbar
Consultants: Dr. Anna Klebanov, Dr. Sindi Sabourin
Editors: Megan Burns, Liane Tsui, Natalie Francis, Annie Chern, Julia Cochrane, Janice Dyer, Laura Edlund, Neomi Majmudar, Una Malcolm, Jodi Rauch
Layout and Illustrations: Linh Lam, Sawyer Paul, Gabriella Kerr
Cover Design: Sunday Lek
Cover Photograph: © Jan Bures/Shutterstock

ISBN 978-1-77395-293-2

First printing January 2024

Parts of this material were first published in 2014 in AP Book 1.1, US edition (978-1-927457-32-0) and AP Book 1.2, US edition (978-1-927457-33-7).

Printed and bound in Canada

Welcome to JUMP Math!

Entering the world of JUMP Math means believing that every learner has the capacity to be fully numerate and love math.

The **JUMP Math Accumula Student Book** is the companion to the **JUMP Math Accumula** supplementary resource for Grades 1 to 8, which is designed to strengthen foundational math knowledge and prepare all students for success in understanding math problems at grade level. This book provides opportunities for students to consolidate learning by exploring important math concepts through independent practice.

Unique Evidence-Based Approach and Resources

JUMP Math's unique approach, Kindergarten to Grade 8 resources, and professional learning for teachers have been producing positive learning outcomes for children and teachers in classrooms in Canada, the United States, and other countries for over 20 years. Our resources are aligned with the science on how children's brains learn best and have been demonstrated through studies to greatly improve problem solving, computation, and fluency skills. (See our research at **jumpmath.org**.) Our approach is designed to build equity by supporting the full spectrum of learners to achieve success in math.

Confidence Building is Key

JUMP Math begins each grade with review to enable every student to quickly develop the confidence needed to engage deeply with math. Our distinctive incremental approach to learning math concepts gradually increases the level of difficulty for students, empowering them to become motivated, independent problem solvers. Our books are also designed with simple pictures and models to avoid overwhelming learners when introducing new concepts, enabling them to see the deep structure of the math and gain the confidence to solve a wide range of math problems.

About JUMP Math

JUMP Math is a non-profit organization dedicated to helping every child in every classroom develop confidence, understanding, and a love of math. JUMP Math also offers a comprehensive set of classroom resources for students in Kindergarten to Grade 8.

For more information, visit JUMP Math at: www.jumpmath.org.

Contents

1. Counting

☐ Color.

1.

3 ants

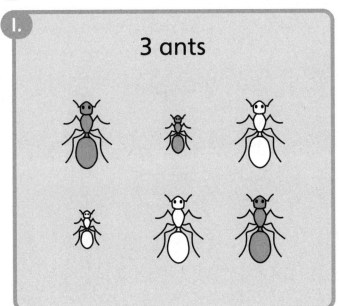

2.

3 ladybugs

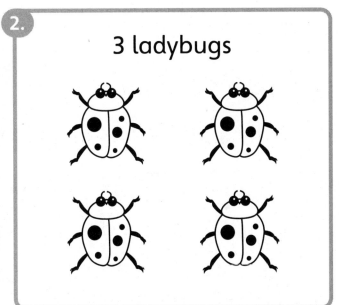

3.

3 bubbles

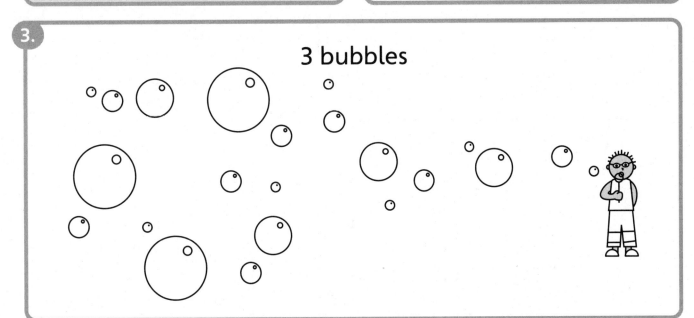

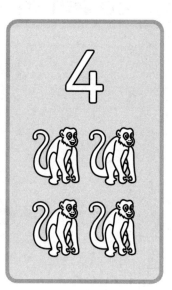

☐ Color.

4. 2 spots

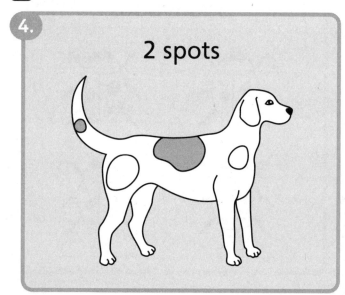

5. 4 spots

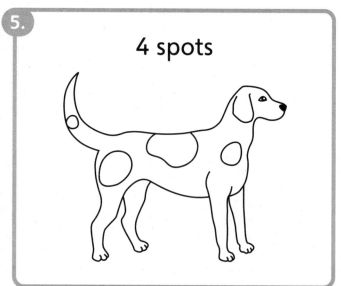

6. 3 spots

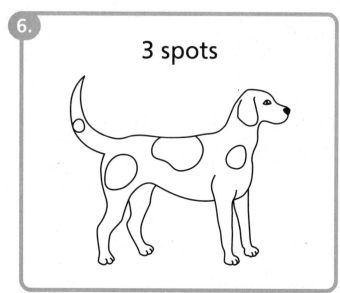

7. I spot

2. Match by Counting

☐ Match by number.

1.

2.

3.

☐ Match by number.

4.

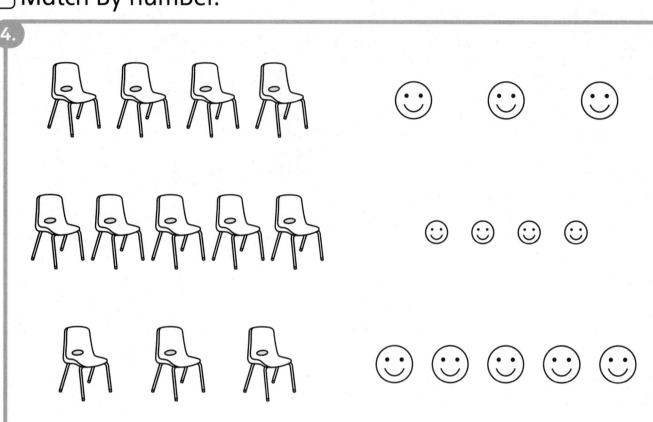

5.

☐ Match by number.

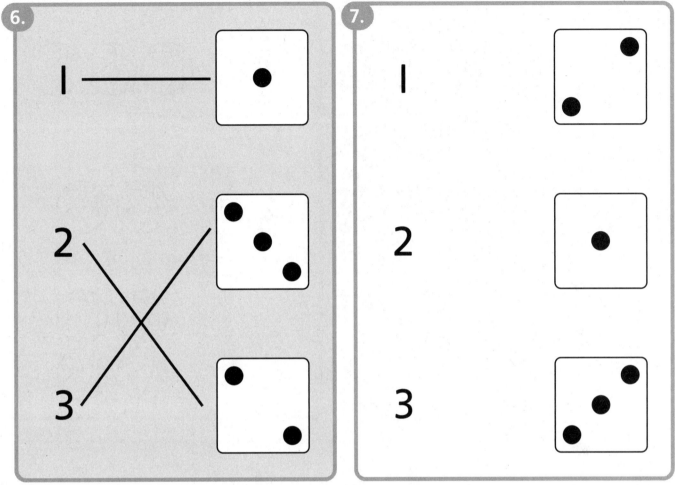

6.

1 ——— [die: 1]

2 ✕ [die: 3]

3 [die: 2]

7.

1 [die: 2]

2 [die: 1]

3 [die: 3]

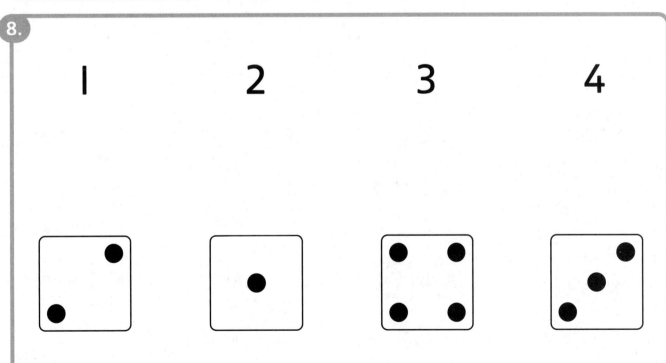

8.

1   2   3   4

[die: 2]   [die: 1]   [die: 4]   [die: 3]

☐ Match by number.

9.

1

3

10.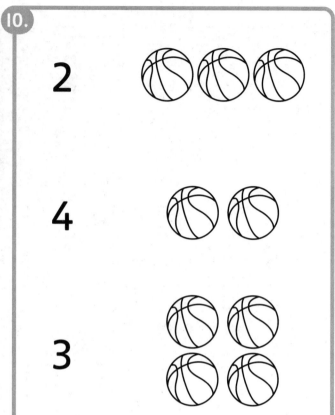

2

4

3

11.

7   q   6   8

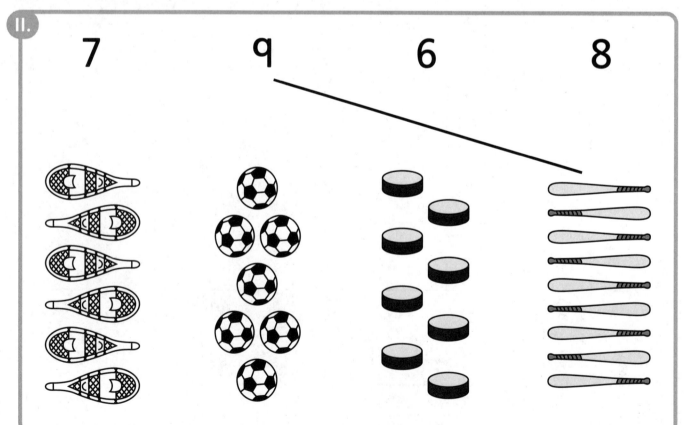

☐ Circle the groups of 5.
☐ Cross out the other groups.

12.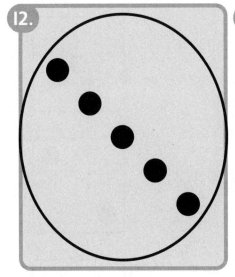

13.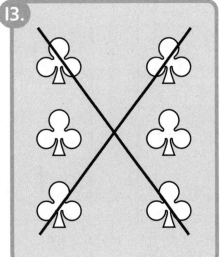

14.

15.

16.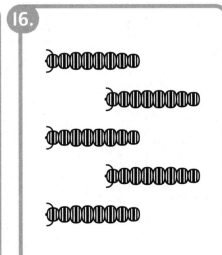

17.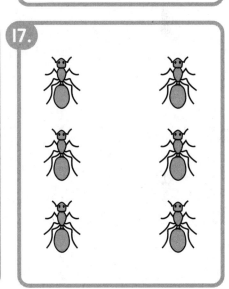

18.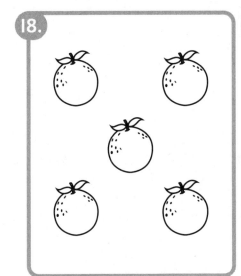

19.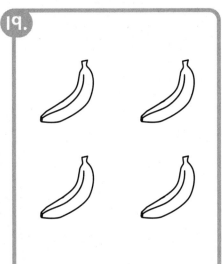

20.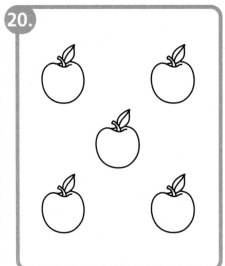

3. Zero

☐ Match by number.

1.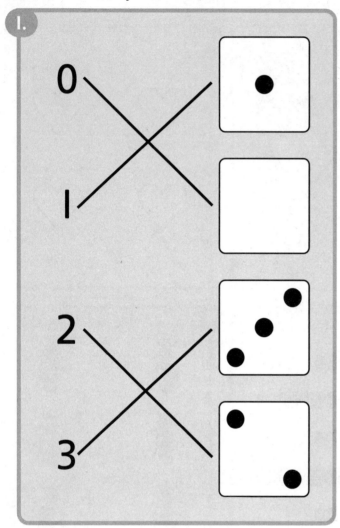

2.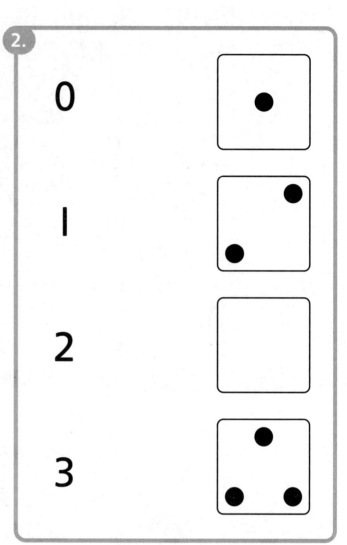

3.

0	1	2	3	4

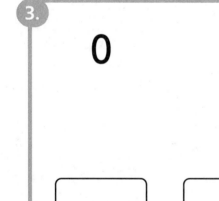   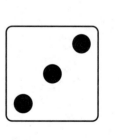

☐ Match by number.

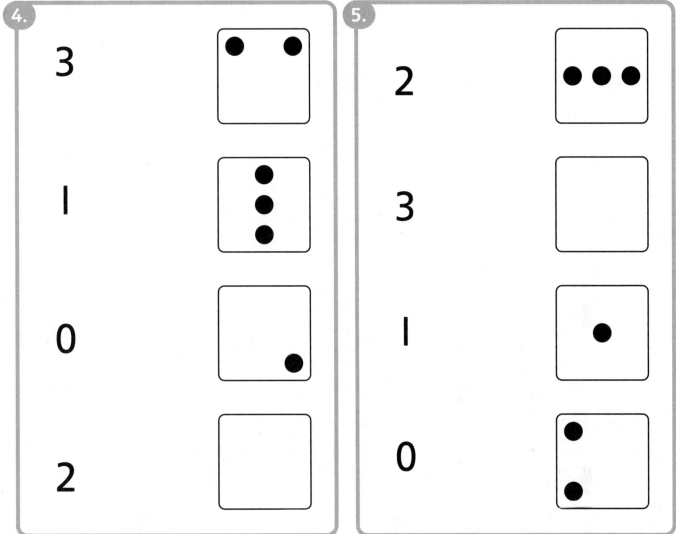

4.

3

1

0

2

5.

2

3

1

0

6.

3   1   4   0   2

☐ Circle.

7. 3 frogs

8. 1 penguin

9. 0 grasshoppers
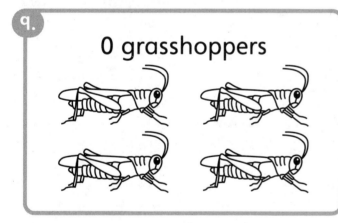

10. 4 bunnies

11. 2 hamsters
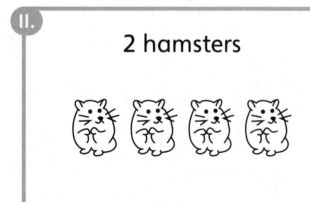

12. 3 bears

JUMP Math Accumula

0 1 2 3 4 5 6 7 8 9

☐ Circle the numbers.

13. (3) ε

14. ᔭ 4

15. 5 ᒫ

16. 6 ᓇ

17. 8 ∞

18. ω 3

19. q d

20. p q

21. 2 S

22. ⌐ 7 Γ ⌐

23. ⌐ q 8 ᔭ

24. BONUS ⌐ 3 0 ∞ ᓇ ᒫ S 0

4. Writing Numbers

☐ Join the dots in order.

1.
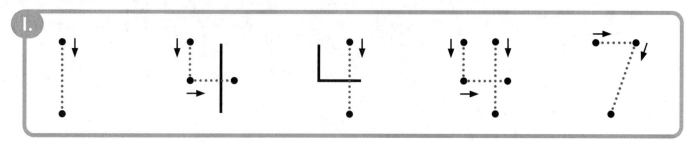

☐ Trace.

2.
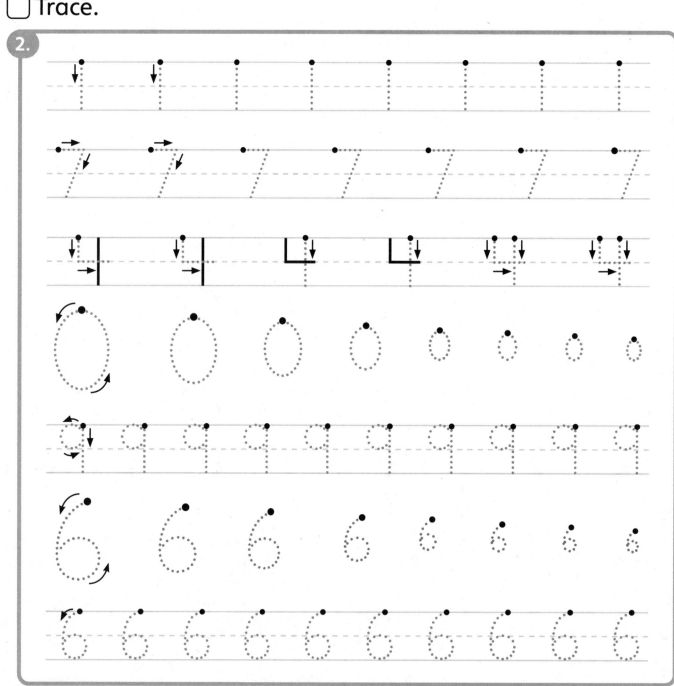

☐ Trace.

3.

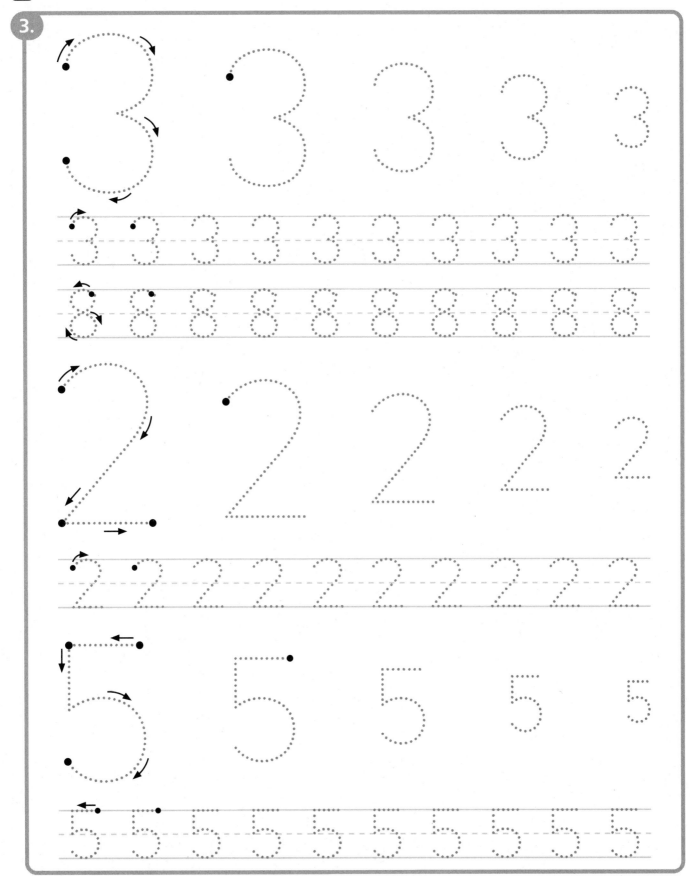

☐ How many legs?

4.

2 4 6 8

5.

2 4 6 8

6.

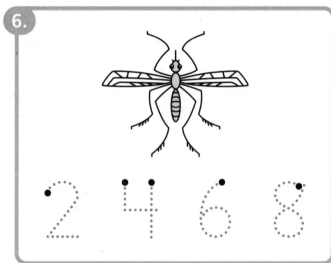

2 4 6 8

7.

2 4 6 8

8.

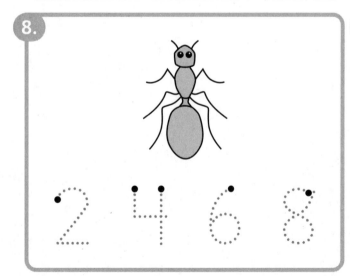

2 4 6 8

9.

2 4 6 8

☐ **BONUS:** Insects have 6 legs. Circle the insects.

5. Counting On

☐ Count the puppies.

1.

_5_ puppies

2.

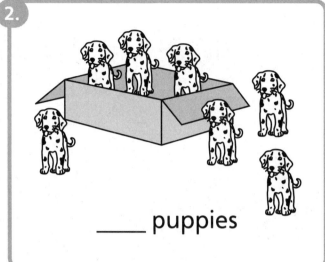

____ puppies

3.

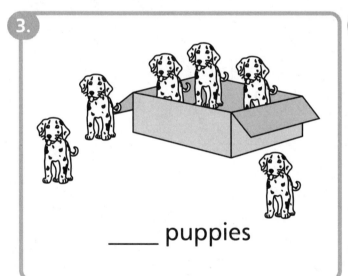

____ puppies

4.

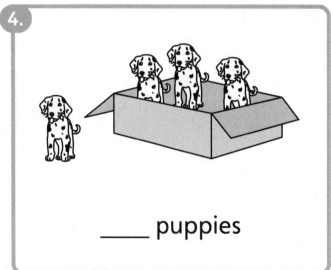

____ puppies

5.

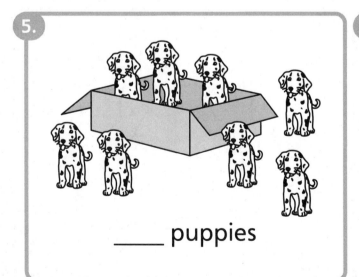

____ puppies

6.

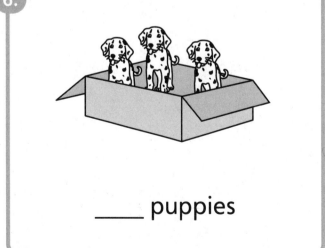

____ puppies

☐ Count the fingers that are up.

7.

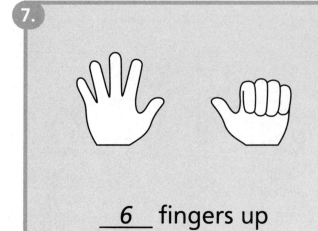

___6___ fingers up

8.

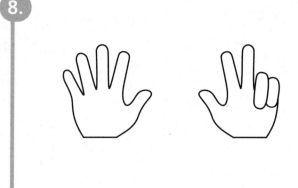

_____ fingers up

9.

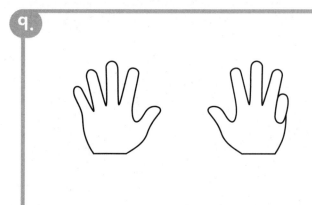

_____ fingers up

10.

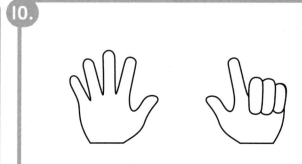

_____ fingers up

11.

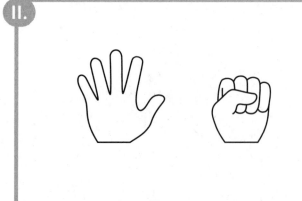

_____ fingers up

12.

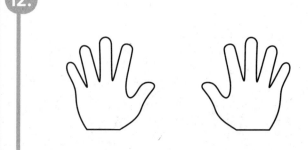

_____ fingers up

6. Counting Using a Chart

☐ Trace the numbers.
☐ How many fish?

1.

There are __5__ fish.

2.

There are ____ fish.

3.

There are ____ fish.

4.

There are ____ fish.

☐ How many ants?

5.

1 2 3 4 5 6 7 8 9 10

There are __6__ ants.

6.

1 2 3 4 5 6 7 8 9 10

There are _____ ants.

7.

1 2 3 4 5 6 7 8 9 10

There are _____ ants.

8.

1 2 3 4 5 6 7 8 9 10

There are _____ ants.

☐ How many blocks?

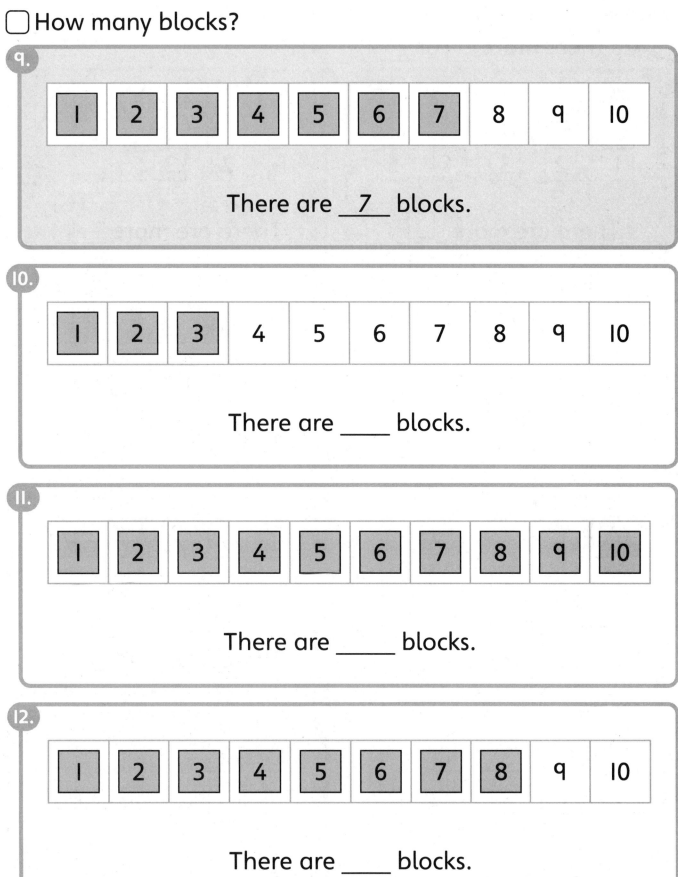

9.

| 1 | 2 | 3 | 4 | 5 | 6 | 7 | 8 | 9 | 10 |

There are __7__ blocks.

10.

| 1 | 2 | 3 | 4 | 5 | 6 | 7 | 8 | 9 | 10 |

There are _____ blocks.

11.

| 1 | 2 | 3 | 4 | 5 | 6 | 7 | 8 | 9 | 10 |

There are _____ blocks.

12.

| 1 | 2 | 3 | 4 | 5 | 6 | 7 | 8 | 9 | 10 |

There are _____ blocks.

7. More and Fewer

 Are there **more** or ?

1.
There are more .

2.
There are more ____.

3.
There are more ____.

4.
There are more ____.

5.
There are more ____.

6.
There are more ____.

7.
There are more ____.

8.
There are more ____.

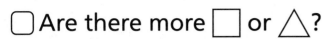 Are there more ☐ or △?

9.

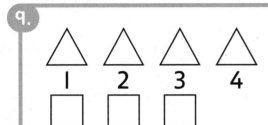

There are more ____.

10.

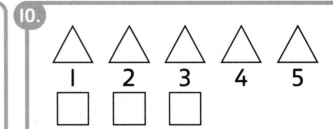

There are more ____.

11.

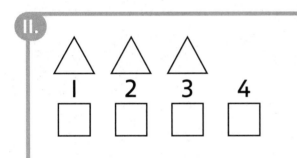

There are more ____.

12.

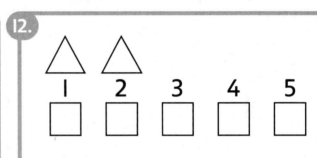

There are more ____.

13.

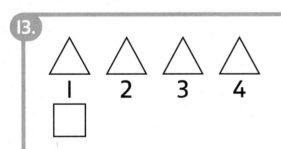

There are more ____.

14.

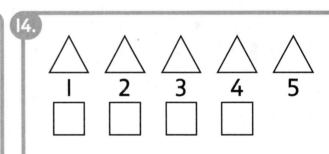

There are more ____.

15.

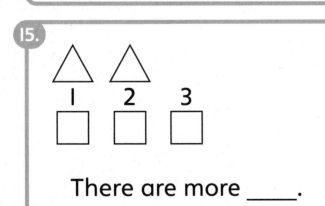

There are more ____.

16.

There are more ____.

Are there **fewer** ☐ or △?

17.

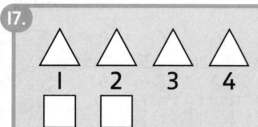

There are fewer ☐.

18.

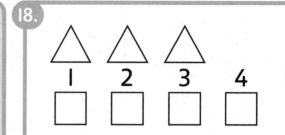

There are fewer ____.

19.

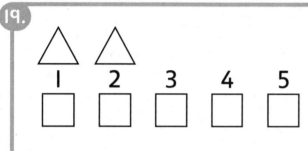

There are fewer ____.

20.

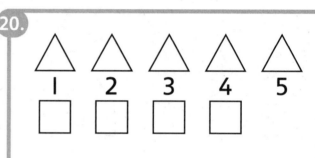

There are fewer ____.

21.

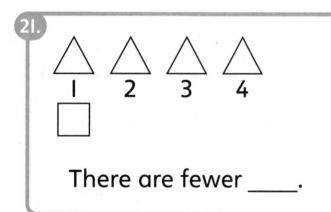

There are fewer ____.

22.

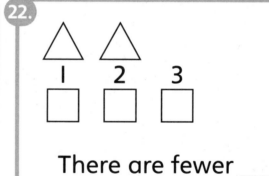

There are fewer ____.

23.

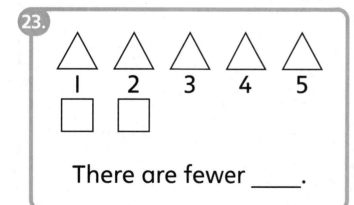

There are fewer ____.

24.

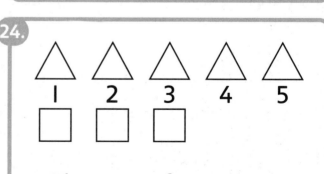

There are fewer ____.

8. Matching

 Pair the ☐ and △.

 Are there more ☐ or △?

1.

There are more ☐.

2.

There are more ____.

3.

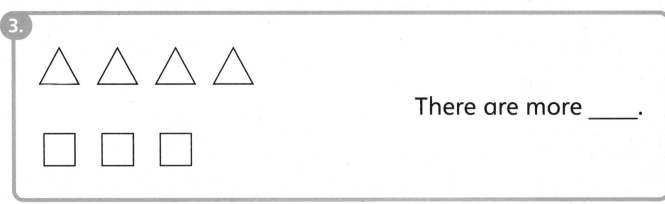

There are more ____.

4.

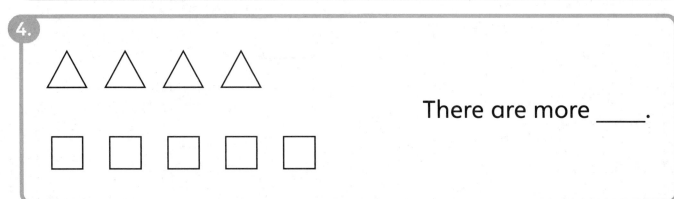

There are more ____.

☐ Can each mouse have a piece of cheese?

5.

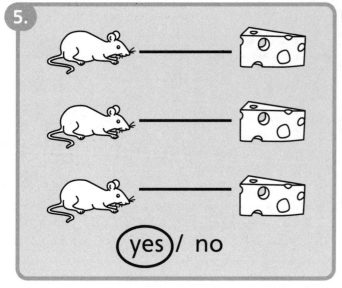

(yes)/ no

6.

yes / no

7.

yes / no

8.

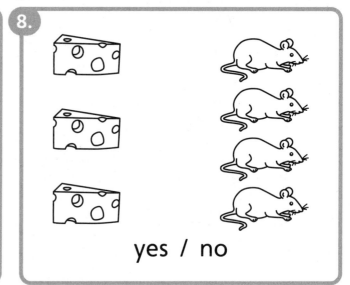

yes / no

9. BONUS

yes / no

Are there more books or people?

10.

books / (people)

11.

books / people

12. BONUS

books / people

13. BONUS

books / people

q. How Many More?

☐ How many more ◯ than △?

1.

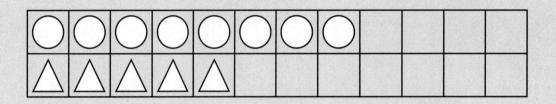

There are ___3___ more ◯ than △.

2.

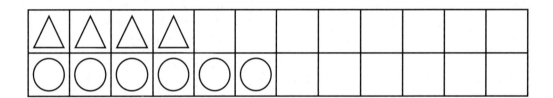

There are ____ more ◯ than △.

3.

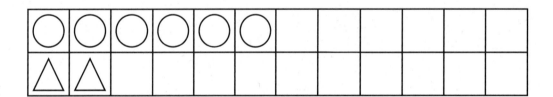

There are ____ more ◯ than △.

4.

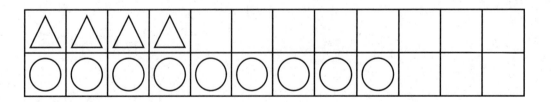

There are ____ more ◯ than △.

☐ Color the extra △.
☐ How many more △ than ◯?

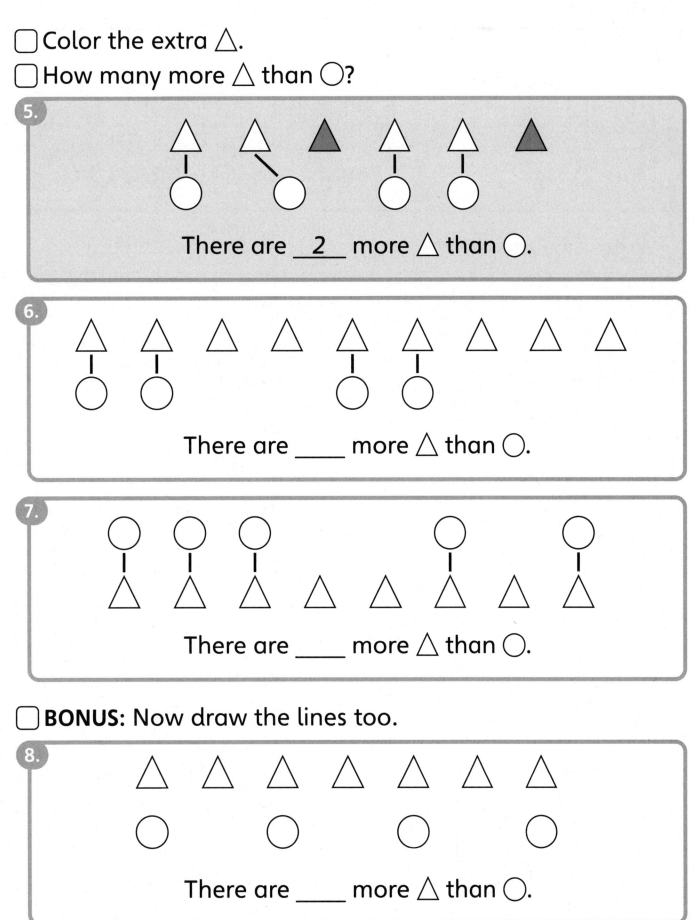

5. There are __2__ more △ than ◯.

6. There are ____ more △ than ◯.

7. There are ____ more △ than ◯.

☐ BONUS: Now draw the lines too.

8. There are ____ more △ than ◯.

10. Equal

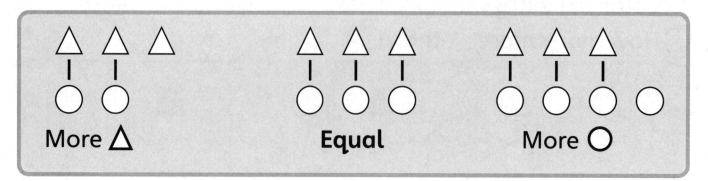

More △   Equal   More ◯

☐ Write ✓ by the answer.

1.

more △   ____

equal △ and ◯   ✓

more ◯   ____

2.

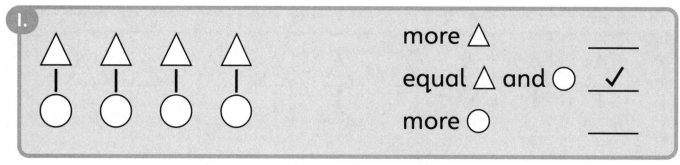

more △   ____

equal △ and ◯   ____

more ◯   ____

3.

more △   ____

equal △ and ◯   ____

more ◯   ____

4.

more △   ____

equal △ and ◯   ____

more ◯   ____

Number the items.

Write ✓ by the answer.

5.

| 1 | 2 | 3 | 4 |

1   2   3

more ☐ ___ ✓

equal ☐ and ○ ___

more ○ ___

6.

more ☐ ___

equal ☐ and ○ ___

more ○ ___

7.

more ☐ ___

equal ☐ and ○ ___

more ○ ___

8.

more ☐ ___

equal ☐ and ○ ___

more ○ ___

9.

more ☐ ___

equal ☐ and ○ ___

more ○ ___

II. Equal and Not Equal with Numbers

☐ Write the number of balls.
☐ Circle **equal** or **not equal**.

1.

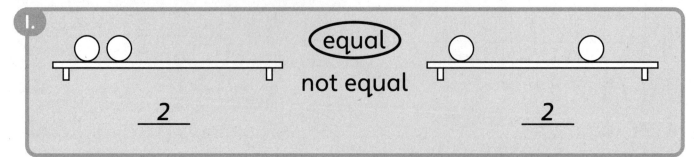

equal

not equal

2

2

2.

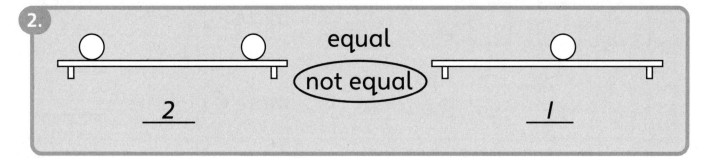

equal

not equal

2

1

3.

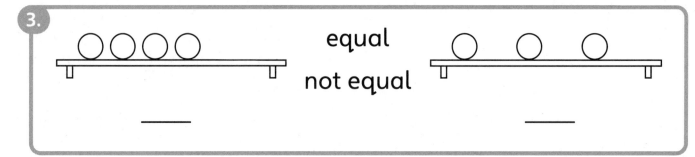

equal

not equal

____

____

4.

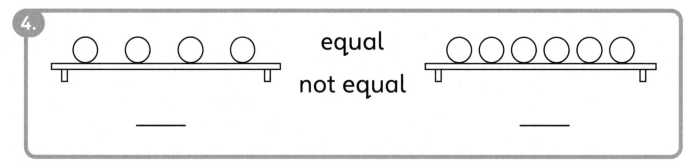

equal

not equal

____

____

5.

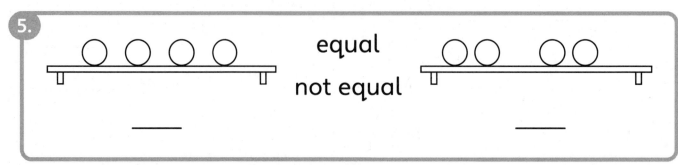

equal

not equal

____

____

☐ Write the number of balls.

☐ Write = if the numbers are the same.

6.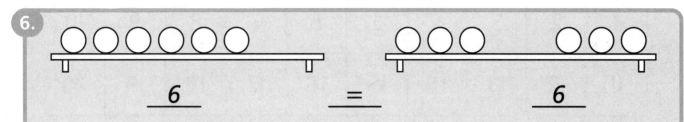

_____ 6 _____   _____ = _____   _____ 6 _____

7.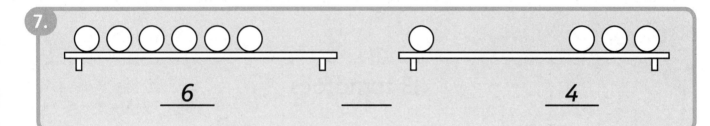

_____ 6 _____   _____   _____ 4 _____

8.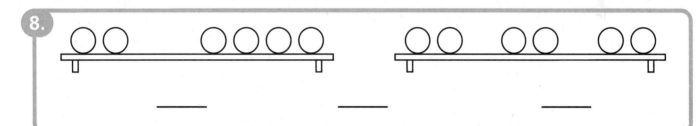

_____   _____   _____

9.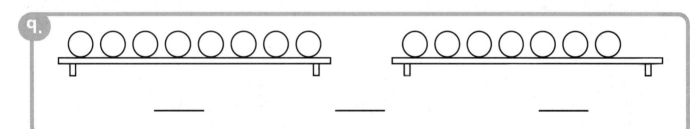

_____   _____   _____

10.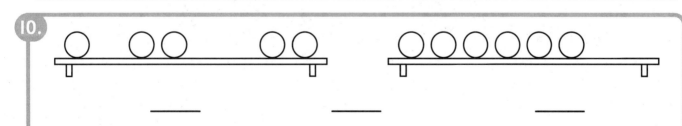

_____   _____   _____

11.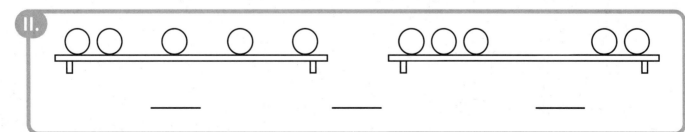

_____   _____   _____

12. Counting to 20

1	2	3	4	5	6	7	8	9	10
11	12	13	14	15	16	17	18	19	20

☐ Circle.

1.

13 tomatoes

2.

12 frogs

3.

15 trees

1	2	3	4	5	6	7	8	9	10
11	12	13	14	15	16	17	18	19	20

☐ How many?

4.

___14___ stars

5.

_____ leaves

6.

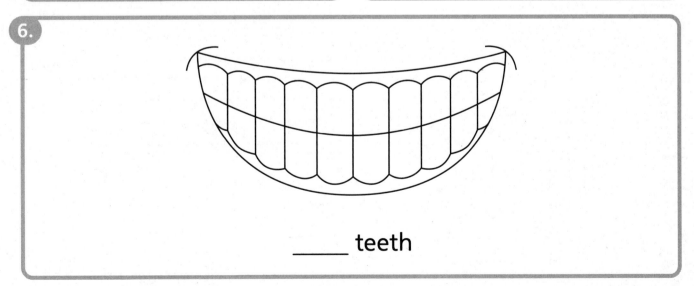

_____ teeth

13. Using a Chart to Count to 20

☐ How many blocks?

1.

1	2	3	4	5	6	7	8	9	10
11	12	13	14	15	16	17	18	19	20

_16_ blocks

2.

1	2	3	4	5	6	7	8	9	10
11	12	13	14	15	16	17	18	19	20

_____ blocks

3.

1	2	3	4	5	6	7	8	9	10
11	12	13	14	15	16	17	18	19	20

_____ blocks

4.

1	2	3	4	5	6	7	8	9	10
11	12	13	14	15	16	17	18	19	20

_____ blocks

☐ Circle the next number in the chart.
☐ Write the number.

5.

1	2	3	④	5	6	7	8	9	10
11	12	13	14	15	16	17	18	19	20

6. 3 _4_

7. 8 ____

8. 16 ____

9.

1	2	3	4	5	6	7	8	9	10
11	12	13	14	15	16	17	18	19	20

10. 5 ____

11. 9 ____

12. 13 ____

13.

1	2	3	4	5	6	7	8	9	10
11	12	13	14	15	16	17	18	19	20

14. 17 ____

15. 2 ____

16. 11 ____

1	2	3	4	5	6	7	8	9	10
11	12	13	14	15	16	17	18	19	20

☐ What comes next?

17.
6 _____

18.
8 _____

19.
17 _____

20.
4 _____

21.
10 _____

22.
19 _____

23.
18 _____

24.
11 _____

25.
9 _____

26.
13 _____

27.
14 _____

28.
15 _____

☐ **BONUS:** Cover the chart.

29.
3 _____

30.
12 _____

31.
16 _____

14. Tens and Ones Blocks

Each circle has 10 bugs.

☐ How many bugs in all?

1.

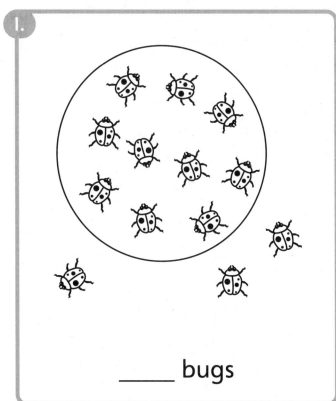

_____ bugs

2.

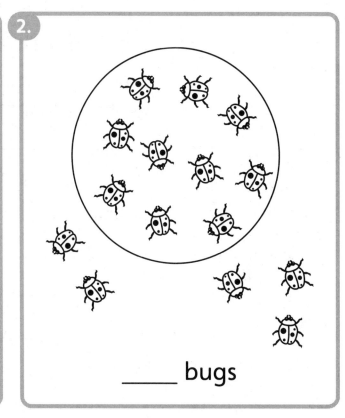

_____ bugs

3.

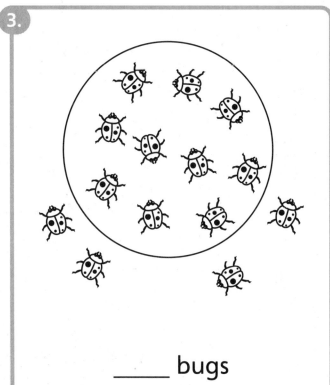

_____ bugs

4.

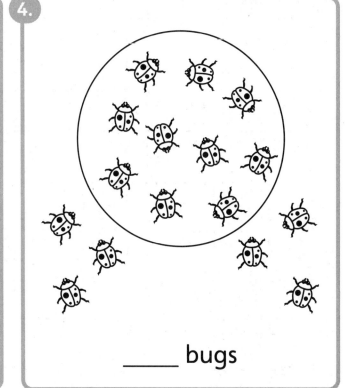

_____ bugs

Ones block   Tens block

There are 10 ones blocks in a tens block.

| 1 | 2 | 3 | 4 | 5 | 6 | 7 | 8 | 9 | 10 |

| 1 | 2 | 3 | 4 | 5 | 6 | 7 | 8 | 9 | 10 |

☐ Count all the blocks.

5.

_13_ blocks in all

6.

____ blocks in all

7.

____ blocks in all

8.

____ blocks in all

JUMP Math Accumula

☐ Count all the blocks.

9.

[row of 10 squares]
[row of 4 squares]   ____ blocks in all

10.

[row of 10 squares]
[row of 6 squares]   ____ blocks in all

11.

[row of 10 squares]
[1 square]   ____ blocks in all

12.

[row of 10 squares]
[row of 8 squares]   ____ blocks in all

13.

[row of 10 squares]
[row of 9 squares]   ____ blocks in all

⬜ Write the numbers that come after 10 in the blocks.

⬜ How many blocks in all?

14.

| 1 | 2 | 3 | 4 | 5 | 6 | 7 | 8 | 9 | 10 |

| 11 | 12 | | | |

_____ blocks in all

15.

| 1 | 2 | 3 | 4 | 5 | 6 | 7 | 8 | 9 | 10 |

| | | |

_____ blocks in all

16.

| 1 | 2 | 3 | 4 | 5 | 6 | 7 | 8 | 9 | 10 |

| | | | |

_____ blocks in all

17.

| 1 | 2 | 3 | 4 | 5 | 6 | 7 | 8 | 9 | 10 |

| | |

_____ blocks in all

15. More Tens and Ones Blocks

☐ Count the **tens blocks** and **ones blocks**.

1.

1	2	3	4	5	6	7	8	9	10
11	12	13	14	15	16	17	18	19	20

18 is __*1*__ tens block and __8__ ones blocks.

2.

1	2	3	4	5	6	7	8	9	10
11	12	13	14	15	16	17	18	19	20

15 is _____ tens block and _____ ones blocks.

3.

1	2	3	4	5	6	7	8	9	10
11	12	13	14	15	16	17	18	19	20

17 is _____ tens block and _____ ones blocks.

4.

1	2	3	4	5	6	7	8	9	10
11	12	13	14	15	16	17	18	19	20

11 is _____ tens block and _____ ones block.

Place a tens block and a ones block on the chart.

☐ How many do you need for each number?

1	2	3	4	5	6	7	8	9	10
11	12	13	14	15	16	17	18	19	20

5.

14 is _____ tens block and _____ ones blocks.

6.

19 is _____ tens block and _____ ones blocks.

7.

16 is _____ tens block and _____ ones blocks.

8.

13 is _____ tens block and _____ ones blocks.

9.

12 is _____ tens block and _____ ones blocks.

10. BONUS

20 is __*1*__ tens block and _____ ones blocks.

Hundreds chart: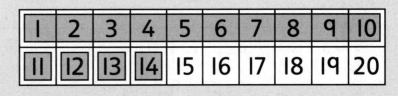

Tens and ones blocks: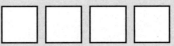

14 is 1 ten and 4 ones.

☐ What number do the blocks show?

11.

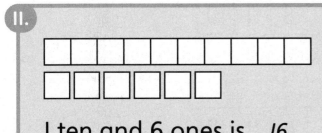

1 ten and 6 ones is __16__.

12.

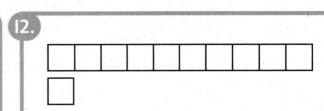

1 ten and 1 one is _____.

13.

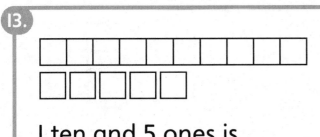

1 ten and 5 ones is _____.

14.

1 ten and 3 ones is _____.

15.

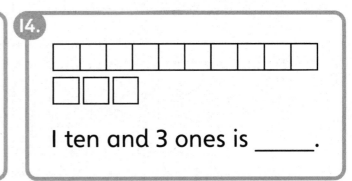

1 ten and 9 ones is _____.

16.

1 ten and 7 ones is _____.

16. Greater Than with Charts

6 is 6 ones. | **1** | **2** | **3** | **4** | **5** | **6** | 7 | 8 | 9 | 10 |

4 is 4 ones. | **1** | **2** | **3** | **4** | 5 | 6 | 7 | 8 | 9 | 10 |

6 is **greater than** 4.

☐ Circle the greater number.

1.

| **1** | **2** | **3** | **4** | **5** | **6** | **7** | 8 | 9 | 10 |

⑦

| **1** | **2** | **3** | 4 | 5 | 6 | 7 | 8 | 9 | 10 |

3

2.

| **1** | **2** | **3** | 4 | 5 | 6 | 7 | 8 | 9 | 10 |

3

| **1** | **2** | **3** | **4** | **5** | 6 | 7 | 8 | 9 | 10 |

5

3.

| **1** | **2** | **3** | **4** | 5 | 6 | 7 | 8 | 9 | 10 |

4

| **1** | **2** | **3** | **4** | **5** | **6** | 7 | 8 | 9 | 10 |

6

4.

| **1** | **2** | **3** | **4** | **5** | **6** | **7** | **8** | **9** | 10 |

9

| **1** | 2 | 3 | 4 | 5 | 6 | 7 | 8 | 9 | 10 |

1

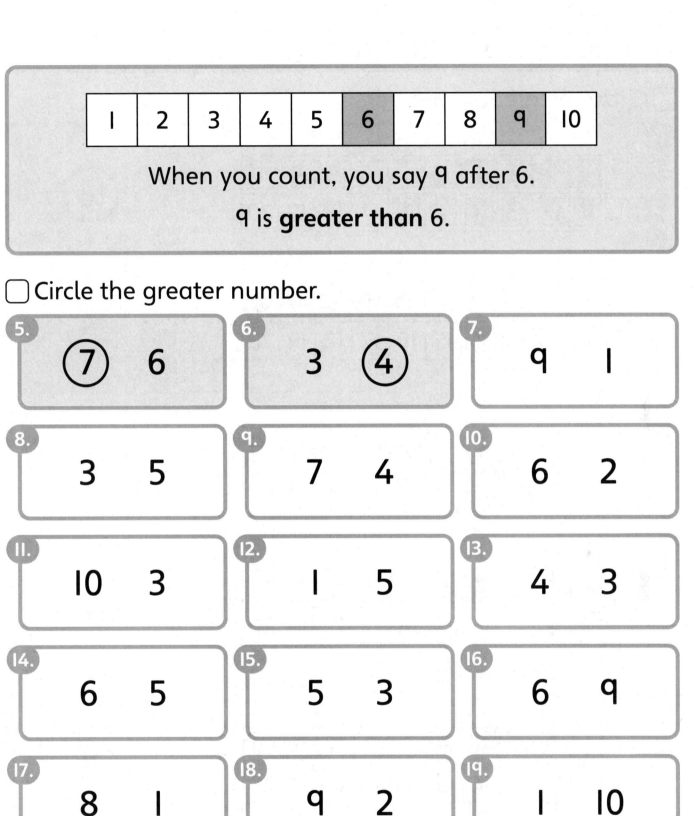

| 1 | 2 | 3 | 4 | 5 | 6 | 7 | 8 | 9 | 10 |

When you count, you say 9 after 6.

9 is **greater than** 6.

☐ Circle the greater number.

5. ⑦ 6

6. 3 ④

7. 9 1

8. 3 5

9. 7 4

10. 6 2

11. 10 3

12. 1 5

13. 4 3

14. 6 5

15. 5 3

16. 6 9

17. 8 1

18. 9 2

19. 1 10

20. 8 10

21. 3 9

22. 7 8

☐ Circle the greater number.

1.

1	2	3	4	5	6	7	8	9	10
11	12	13	14	15	16	17	18	19	20

⑯

1	2	3	4	5	6	7	8	9	10
11	12	13	14	15	16	17	18	19	20

14

2.

1	2	3	4	5	6	7	8	9	10
11	12	13	14	15	16	17	18	19	20

17

1	2	3	4	5	6	7	8	9	10
11	12	13	14	15	16	17	18	19	20

12

3.

1	2	3	4	5	6	7	8	9	10
11	12	13	14	15	16	17	18	19	20

11

1	2	3	4	5	6	7	8	9	10
11	12	13	14	15	16	17	18	19	20

15

1	2	3	4	5	6	7	8	9	10
11	12	13	14	15	16	17	18	19	20

When you count, you say 15 after 12.

15 is greater than 12.

☐ Circle the greater number.

4. 12 (14)

5. 11 15

6. 20 15

7. 13 19

8. 14 17

9. 8 9

10. 11 9

11. 12 10

12. 15 8

13. 20 16

14. 13 14

15. 14 19

16. 1 19

17. 2 18

18. 3 7

19. 6 12

20. 7 13

21. 16 4

1	2	3	4	5	6	7	8	9	10
11	12	13	14	15	16	17	18	19	20

☐ Circle the numbers that are greater than 10.

22.

5   12   7   13   2   18

☐ Circle the greater number.

23.

10   2

24.

3   10

25.

10   17

26.

5   10

27.

16   10

28.

13   10

☐ Circle the greater number.

29.

5   11

30.

17   4

31.

3   12

32.

8   16

33.

13   5

34.

19   1

18. Adding

 Add by counting.

1.

4   +   3   =   _____

2.

3   +   5   =   _____

3.

   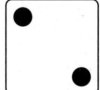

5   +   2   =   _____

4.

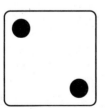   

2   +   6   =   _____

☐ Draw circles to add.

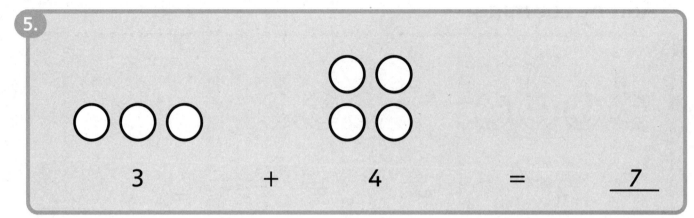

5.

○ ○ ○   ○ ○
              ○ ○

3   +   4   =   _7_

6.

2   +   3   =   ____

7.

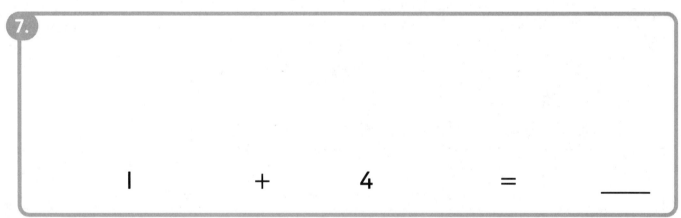

1   +   4   =   ____

8.

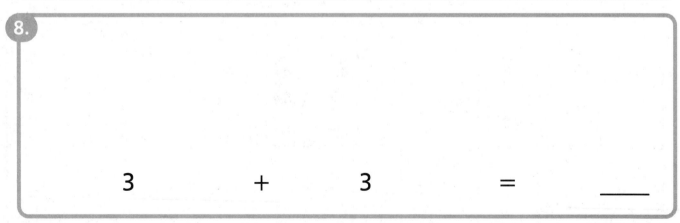

3   +   3   =   ____

How many in total?

9.

3 flags   +   2 flags   =   _____ flags in total

3 balls   +   2 balls   =   _____ balls in total

$$3 + 2 = \text{\_\_\_\_}$$

10.

_____ trees in total   =   2 trees   +   4 trees

_____ children   =   2 girls   +   4 boys

$$\text{\_\_\_\_} = 2 + 4$$

19. More Adding

☐ Add.

1.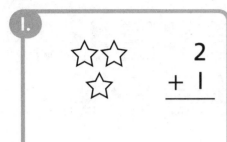
$$\begin{array}{r} 2 \\ + 1 \\ \hline \end{array}$$

2.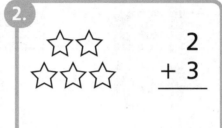
$$\begin{array}{r} 2 \\ + 3 \\ \hline \end{array}$$

3.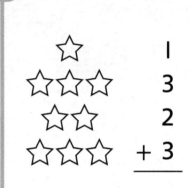
$$\begin{array}{r} 1 \\ 3 \\ 2 \\ + 3 \\ \hline \end{array}$$

4.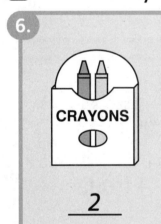
$$\begin{array}{r} 2 \\ + 2 \\ \hline \end{array}$$

5.
$$\begin{array}{r} 1 \\ + 4 \\ \hline \end{array}$$

☐ How many crayons in all?

6.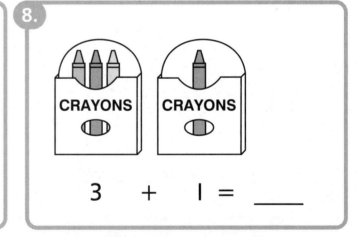

$\underline{\quad 2 \quad}$

7.

$\underline{\quad\quad}$

8.

$3 \ + \ 1 = \underline{\quad\quad}$

9.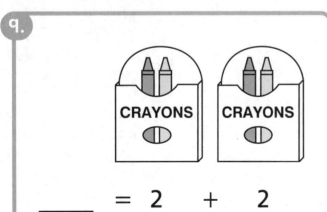

$\underline{\quad\quad} = 2 \ + \ 2$

10.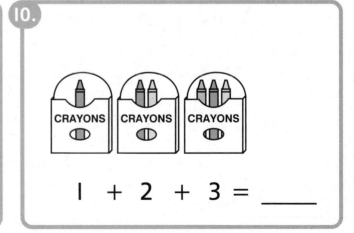

$1 \ + \ 2 \ + \ 3 = \underline{\quad\quad}$

☐ Draw a picture to add.

11.

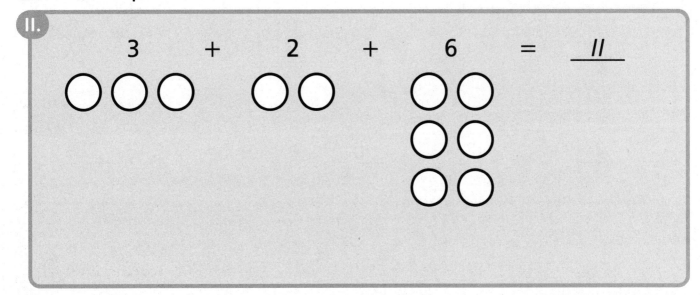

$$3 \quad + \quad 2 \quad + \quad 6 \quad = \quad \underline{11}$$

12.

$$4 \quad + \quad 2 \quad + \quad 3 \quad = \quad \underline{}$$

13.

$$
\begin{array}{r}
3 \\
2 \\
+\ 5 \\
\hline
\end{array}
$$

14.

$$
\begin{array}{r}
4 \\
2 \\
+\ 7 \\
\hline
\end{array}
$$

☐ Add 0.

15.

$$\underline{3} \quad + \quad \underline{0} \quad = \quad \underline{3}$$

16.

$$\underline{} \quad + \quad \underline{} \quad = \quad \underline{}$$

17.

$$\underline{} \quad = \quad \underline{} \quad + \quad \underline{}$$

18.

$$\underline{} \quad = \quad \underline{} \quad + \quad \underline{}$$

19. BONUS

$$0 + 17 = \underline{}$$

20. BONUS

$$\underline{} = 14 + 0$$

JUMP Math Accumula

20. Counting On to Add 1 or 2

☐ Shade the **next** circle.

☐ Add 1.

1.

1 2 3 4

3 + 1 = __4__

2.

1 2 3 4 5

4 + 1 = _____

3.

1 2 3

2 + 1 = _____

4.

1 2 3 4 5 6

5 + 1 = _____

5.

1 2 3 4 5 6 7 8 9 10

7 + 1 = _____

6.

1 2 3 4 5 6 7 8 9 10

8 + 1 = _____

☐ Find the **next** number.

☐ Add 1.

7.

1 2 3 **4** 5

4 + 1 = _5_

8.

1 2 **3** 4 5

3 + 1 = ____

9.

1 2 3 4 **5** 6 7

5 + 1 = ____

10.

1 2 3 4 5 **6** 7

6 + 1 = ____

11.

1 2 3 4 5 6 7 8 9 10

7 + 1 = ____

12.

1 2 3 4 5 6 7 8 9 10

9 + 1 = ____

13.

2 + 1 = ____

14.

8 + 1 = ____

15. BONUS

14 + 1 = ____

☐ Find the **next 2** numbers.

☐ Add 2.

16.

1 2 3 **4** 5 6 7

4 + 2 = _6_

17.

1 2 **3** 4 5 6 7

3 + 2 = ____

18.

1 2 3 4 5 **6** 7 8

6 + 2 = ____

19.

1 2 3 4 **5** 6 7 8

5 + 2 = ____

20.

1 2 3 4 5 6 7 8 9 10 11 12

8 + 2 = ____

21.

1 2 3 4 5 6 7 8 9 10 11 12

9 + 2 = ____

22.

2 + 2 = ____

23.

10 + 2 = ____

24. BONUS

17 + 2 = ____

Add by counting on.

1.

5   _6_   _7_   5 + 2 = _7_

2.

4   ___   ___   ___   4 + 3 = ___

3.

6   ___ ___ ___ ___   6 + 4 = ___

4.

7   ___ ___ ___ ___   7 + 4 = ___

5.

8   ___ ___   8 + 2 = ___

6.   **7.**   **8.**

5 + 3 = ___   3 + 5 = ___   7 + 3 = ___

There are **5** apples in the bag.

☐ Add by counting on.

q.

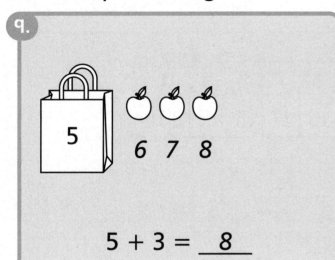

5 + 3 = __8__

10.

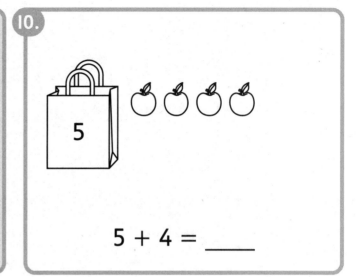

5 + 4 = ___

11.

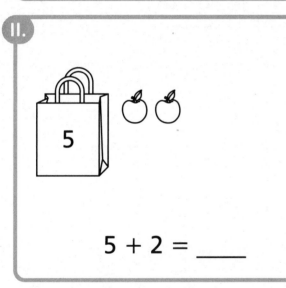

5 + 2 = ___

12.

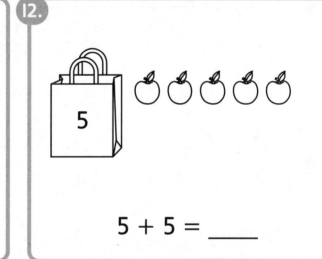

5 + 5 = ___

13.

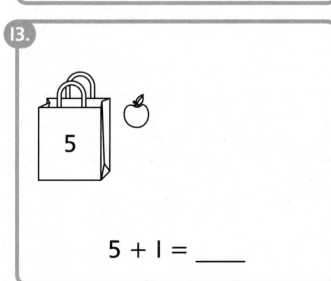

5 + 1 = ___

14.

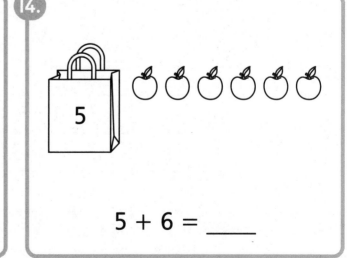

5 + 6 = ___

22. Adding 10

☐ Shade the next 10 numbers.

☐ Add 10.

1.

1	2	3	4	5	6	7	8	9	10
11	12	13	14	15	16	17	18	19	20

$$4 + 10 = \underline{\ 14\ }$$

2.

1	2	3	4	5	6	7	8	9	10
11	12	13	14	15	16	17	18	19	20

$$9 + 10 = \underline{\qquad}$$

3.

1	2	3	4	5	6	7	8	9	10
11	12	13	14	15	16	17	18	19	20

$$1 + 10 = \underline{\qquad}$$

4.

1	2	3	4	5	6	7	8	9	10
11	12	13	14	15	16	17	18	19	20

$$8 + 10 = \underline{\qquad}$$

☐ Look down a row to add 10.

| 1 | 2 | 3 | 4 | 5 | 6 | 7 | 8 | 9 | 10 |
| 11 | 12 | 13 | 14 | 15 | 16 | 17 | 18 | 19 | 20 |

5. $2 + 10 =$ _____

6. $7 + 10 =$ _____

7. $9 + 10 =$ _____

8. $6 + 10 =$ _____

9. $1 + 10 =$ _____

10. $5 + 10 =$ _____

11. $10 + 10 =$ _____

12. $8 + 10 =$ _____

13. $3 + 10 =$ _____

☐ **BONUS:** Cover the rest of the page.

14. $7 + 10 =$ _____

15. $9 + 10 =$ _____

16. $4 + 10 =$ _____

17. $5 + 10 =$ _____

18. $2 + 10 =$ _____

19. $1 + 10 =$ _____

20. $6 + 10 =$ _____

21. $8 + 10 =$ _____

22. $10 + 10 =$ _____

The basket has 10 apples.

☐ How many apples are there in all?

23.
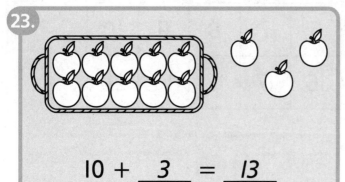

$10 + \underline{\ 3\ } = \underline{\ 13\ }$

24.
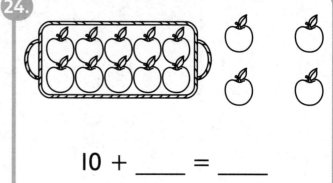

$10 + \underline{\ \ \ } = \underline{\ \ \ }$

25.
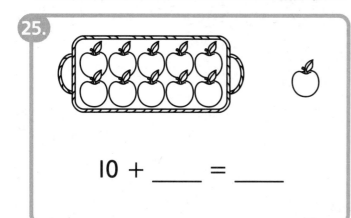

$10 + \underline{\ \ \ } = \underline{\ \ \ }$

26.
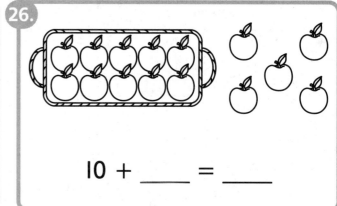

$10 + \underline{\ \ \ } = \underline{\ \ \ }$

☐ Add.

27.
$10 + 2 = \underline{\ \ \ }$

28.
$10 + 7 = \underline{\ \ \ }$

29.
$10 + 6 = \underline{\ \ \ }$

30.
$10 + 8 = \underline{\ \ \ }$

31.
$$\begin{array}{r} 10 \\ + \ 5 \\ \hline \end{array}$$

32.
$$\begin{array}{r} 10 \\ + \ 3 \\ \hline \end{array}$$

33.
$$\begin{array}{r} 10 \\ + \ 4 \\ \hline \end{array}$$

34.
$$\begin{array}{r} 10 \\ + \ 1 \\ \hline \end{array}$$

35.
$$\begin{array}{r} 10 \\ + \ 9 \\ \hline \end{array}$$

23. Pairs That Add to 5 or 10

3	+	2	=	5
fingers up		fingers not up		in all

☐ Use your fingers to find the missing number.

1. $1 + \boxed{} = 5$

2. $4 + \boxed{} = 5$

3. $\boxed{} + 3 = 5$

4. $2 + \boxed{} = 5$

5. $\boxed{} + 2 = 5$

6. $\boxed{} + 1 = 5$

7.
$$\begin{array}{r} 2 \\ + \boxed{} \\ \hline 5 \end{array}$$

8.
$$\begin{array}{r} \boxed{} \\ + \quad 1 \\ \hline 5 \end{array}$$

9.
$$\begin{array}{r} \boxed{} \\ + \quad 3 \\ \hline 5 \end{array}$$

10.
$$\begin{array}{r} 5 \\ + \boxed{} \\ \hline 5 \end{array}$$

11. BONUS $2 + 3 = \boxed{} + 4$

12. BONUS $3 + 2 = \boxed{} + 5$

13. BONUS $4 + 1 = 3 + \boxed{}$

14. BONUS $2 + \boxed{} = 4 + 1$

7	+	3	=	10
up		not up		in all

☐ Use your fingers to find the missing number.

15. 4 + ☐ = 10

16. 5 + ☐ = 10

17. 2 + ☐ = 10

18. ☐ + 7 = 10

19. ☐ + 5 = 10

20. ☐ + 1 = 10

21.
$$\begin{array}{r} 8 \\ + \;\square \\ \hline 10 \end{array}$$

22.
$$\begin{array}{r} 3 \\ + \;\square \\ \hline 10 \end{array}$$

23.
$$\begin{array}{r} \square \\ + \;9 \\ \hline 10 \end{array}$$

24.
$$\begin{array}{r} 10 \\ + \;\square \\ \hline 10 \end{array}$$

25. BONUS
7 + 3 = ☐ + 4

26. BONUS
2 + 8 = ☐ + 5

27. BONUS
☐ + 9 = 3 + 7

28. BONUS
10 + ☐ = 6 + 4

24. Using 10 to Add

☐ Circle two numbers that add to 10.

1.
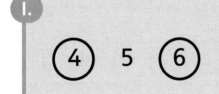
④ 5 ⑥

2.
3 7 9

3.
1 8 9

4.
4 5 5

5.
2 3 8

6.
3 6 4

☐ Circle two numbers that add to 10.
☐ Write the number that is left over.

7.
⑧ + ② + 5 = 10 + $\boxed{5}$

8.
4 + 6 + 3 = 10 + $\boxed{}$

9.
2 + 9 + 1 = 10 + $\boxed{}$

10.
6 + 7 + 4 = 10 + $\boxed{}$

11.
4 + 3 + 7 = 10 + $\boxed{}$

◻ Circle two numbers that add to 10.
◻ Use 10 to add.

12.
(8) + 3 + (2)
= 10 + [3]
= [13]

13.
2 + (7) + (3)
= 10 + ☐
= ☐

14.
1 + 8 + 9
= 10 + ☐
= ☐

15.
3 + 7 + 4
= 10 + ☐
= ☐

16.
4 + 5 + 6
= 10 + ☐
= ☐

17.
5 + 5 + 6
= 10 + ☐
= ☐

18.
9 + 2 + 1
= 10 + ☐
= ☐

19.
3 + 2 + 8
= 10 + ☐
= ☐

20.
4 + 5 + 5
= 10 + ☐
= ☐

21.
8 + 4 + 2
= 10 + ☐
= ☐

22.
7 + 3 + 9
= 10 + ☐
= ☐

23.
6 + 4 + 8
= 10 + ☐
= ☐

25. Doubles

☐ Write a doubles sentence.

1.

4 + 4 = __8__

2.

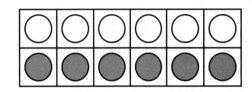

6 + 6 = ____

3.

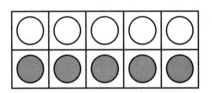

5 + 5 = ____

4.

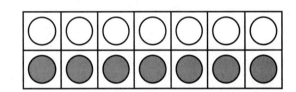

7 + 7 = ____

5.

2 + 2 = ____

6.

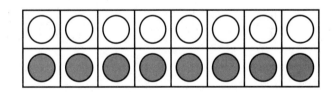

8 + 8 = ____

7.

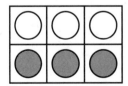

3 + 3 = ____

8.

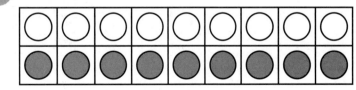

9 + 9 = ____

☐ Draw circles to double the number.

9.

Double 3 is __6__.

3 + 3 = ____

10.

Double 4 is ____.

4 + 4 = ____

11.

Double 2 is ____.

2 + 2 = ____

12.

Double 5 is ____.

5 + 5 = ____

13.

Double 8 is ____.

8 + 8 = ____

14.

Double 7 is ____.

7 + 7 = ____

Fill in the boxes.

15.

$1 + 1 =$ ☐ $6 + 6 =$ ☐

$2 + 2 =$ ☐ $7 + 7 =$ ☐

$3 + 3 =$ ☐ $8 + 8 =$ ☐

$4 + 4 =$ ☐ $9 + 9 =$ ☐

$5 + 5 =$ ☐ $10 + 10 =$ ☐

Fill in the blanks.

16.

Tim has 2 cats.

Jane has 2 cats.

They have ____ + ____ = ____ cats altogether.

17.

Sun has 4 blocks.

Bill has 4 blocks.

They have ____ + ____ = ____ blocks altogether.

26. Using Doubles to Add

 Fill in the blanks.

1.

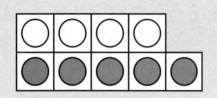   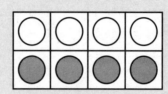

$4 + 5$ $=$ $\underline{\ 4\ }$ $+$ $\underline{\ 4\ }$ $+$ $\underline{\ 1\ }$

2.

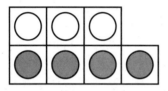   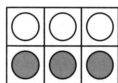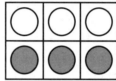

$3 + 4$ $=$ $\underline{\ \ \ \ }$ $+$ $\underline{\ \ \ \ }$ $+$ $\underline{\ \ \ \ }$

3.

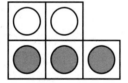

$2 + 3$ $=$ $\underline{\ \ \ \ }$ $+$ $\underline{\ \ \ \ }$ $+$ $\underline{\ \ \ \ }$

4.

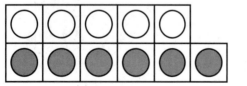   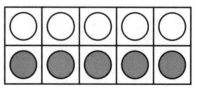

$5 + 6$ $=$ $\underline{\ \ \ \ }$ $+$ $\underline{\ \ \ \ }$ $+$ $\underline{\ \ \ \ }$

☐ Circle the smaller number.
☐ Write the double of the smaller number and add 1.

5.
5 + ④

= _4_ + _4_ + _1_

6.
⑤ + 6

= _5_ + _5_ + _1_

7.
3 + 4

= ___ + ___ + ___

8.
8 + 7

= ___ + ___ + ___

9.
7 + 6

= ___ + ___ + ___

10.
4 + 3

= ___ + ___ + ___

☐ Fill in the blanks.

11.
4 + 5

= 4 + 4 + 1

= ___ + 1

= ___

12.
6 + 7

= 6 + 6 + 1

= ___ + 1

= ___

☐ Add.

13.   3 + 4   **14.**   6 + 5   **15.**   8 + 9   **16.**   7 + 8

27. Addition Word Problems

☐ Add. Use the pictures to help you.

1.

$3 + 2 = \boxed{}$

3 flowers   2 more flowers

2.

$5 + 3 = \boxed{}$

5 flowers   3 more flowers

3.

$4 + 4 = \boxed{}$

4 flowers   4 more flowers

4.

$3 + 6 = \boxed{}$

3 flowers   6 more flowers

5.

$2 + 5 = \boxed{}$

2 flowers   5 more flowers

☐ Draw a picture to add.
☐ Write the number sentence.

6.

2 trees   7 more trees

2 + 7 = 9

7.

5 pencils   4 more pencils

☐ + ☐ = ☐

8.

6 baseballs   5 more baseballs

☐ + ☐ = ☐

☐ Draw circles to help you add.

9.

3 flies are buzzing.   2 join them.

◯ ◯ ◯   ◯ ◯

How many flies altogether?

3 + 2 = ☐ 5

10.

Emma has 4 cats.   John has 2 cats.

How many cats altogether?

4 + 2 = ☐

11.

Rob has 5 oranges.   Tina has 3 oranges.

How many oranges altogether?

☐ + ☐ = ☐

12.

Sara has 4 fish.   Tom has 4 fish.

How many fish altogether?

☐ + ☐ = ☐

Draw circles to solve the problem.

13.
There are 5 small turtles.

There are 6 big turtles.

How many turtles are there altogether?

$\Box + \Box = \Box$

14.
8 children are playing soccer.

5 children join them.

How many are playing soccer now?

$\Box + \Box = \Box$

15.
There are 7 big tables.

There are 6 small tables.

How many tables are there altogether?

$\Box + \Box = \Box$

28. Subtracting

☐ Take away.

1.

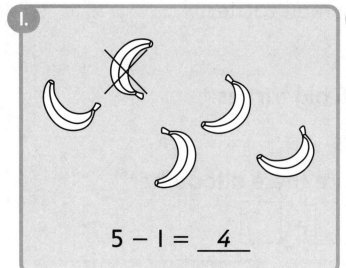

$5 - 1 = \underline{\quad 4 \quad}$

2.

$4 - 1 = \underline{\quad\quad}$

3.

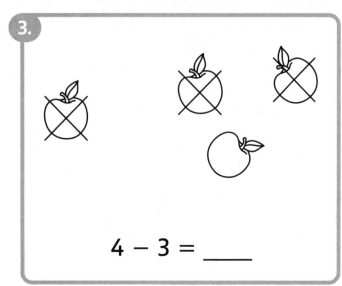

$4 - 3 = \underline{\quad\quad}$

4.

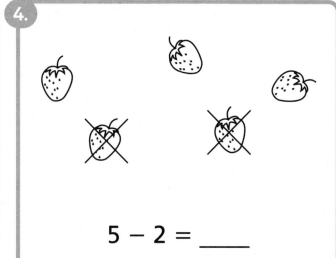

$5 - 2 = \underline{\quad\quad}$

5.

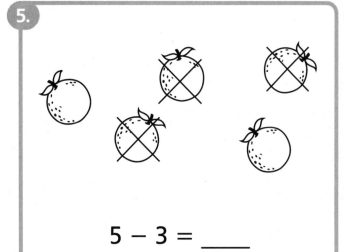

$5 - 3 = \underline{\quad\quad}$

6.

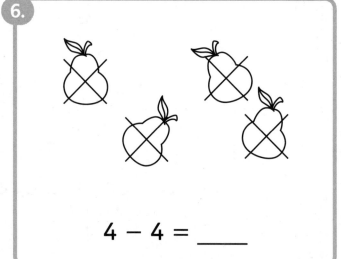

$4 - 4 = \underline{\quad\quad}$

☐ Cross out the correct number.
☐ Subtract.

7.

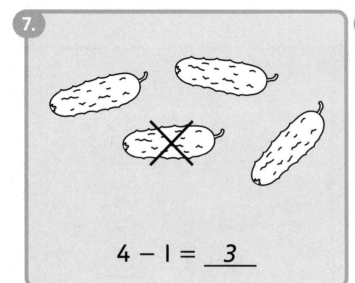

4 − 1 = _3_

8.

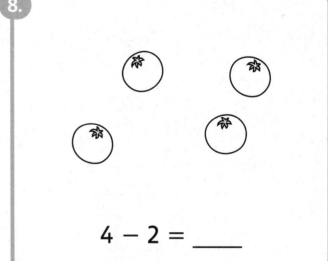

4 − 2 = ____

9.

5 − 3 = ____

10.

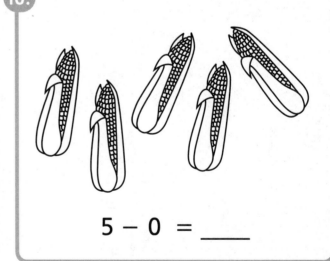

5 − 0 = ____

11.

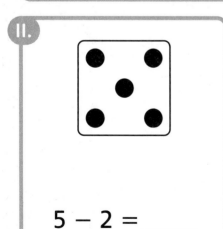

5 − 2 = ____

12.

4 − 3 = ____

13.

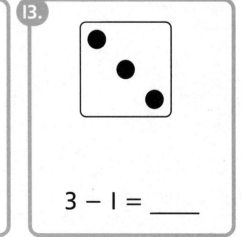

3 − 1 = ____

☐ Draw the first number of circles.
☐ Cross out the second number of circles.
☐ Subtract.

14.

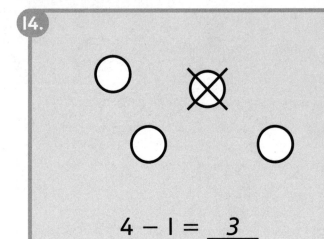

$4 - 1 = \underline{3}$

15.

$5 - 3 = \underline{}$

16.

$4 - 2 = \underline{}$

17.

$6 - 5 = \underline{}$

18.

$3 - 3 = \underline{}$

19.

$4 - 0 = \underline{}$

Eric has 10 apples.

Kim takes away 4 apples.

☐ How many are left?

20.
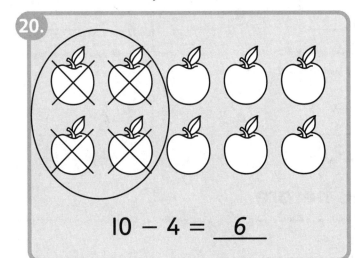

10 − 4 = __6__

21.
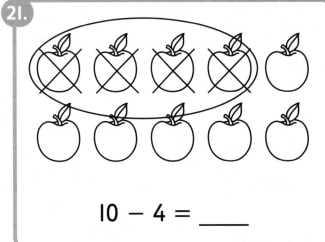

10 − 4 = ____

22.
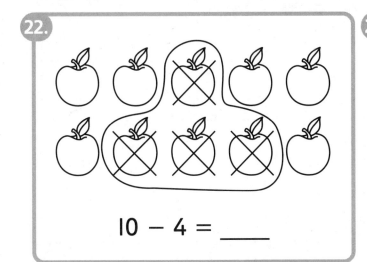

10 − 4 = ____

23.
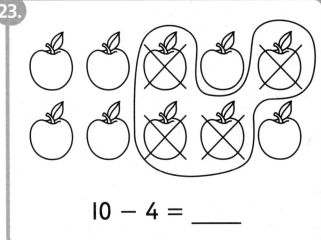

10 − 4 = ____

☐ Take away any 4 apples.

☐ How many are left?

24.

10 − 4 = ____

29. Counting Back

Write the number that comes **after**.

1. 3 __4__	**2.** 4 ___	**3.** 9 ___	**4.** 8 ___	**5.** 2 ___
6. 1 ___	**7.** 0 ___	**8.** 7 ___	**9.** 5 ___	**10.** 6 ___

Write the number that comes **before**.

11. __2__ 3 4 5	**12.** ___ 4 5 6	**13.** ___ 6 7 8

14. ___ 2 3	**15.** ___ 6 7	**16.** ___ 3 4	**17.** ___ 5 6

Write the number that comes **after**.
Write the number that comes **before**.

18. __7__ 8 __9__	**19.** ___ 7 ___	**20.** ___ 5 ___
21. ___ 3 ___	**22.** ___ 4 ___	**23.** ___ 9 ___
24. ___ 2 ___	**25.** ___ 6 ___	**26. BONUS** ___ 10 ___

☐ Write the number that comes before.

27. _7_ 8 9

28. ___ 4 5

29. ___ 2 3

30. ___ 18 19

31. ___ 14 15

32. ___ 12 13

33. ___ 16 17

34. ___ 11 12

35. ___ 19 20

☐ Write the number that comes before.
☐ Write the number that comes after.

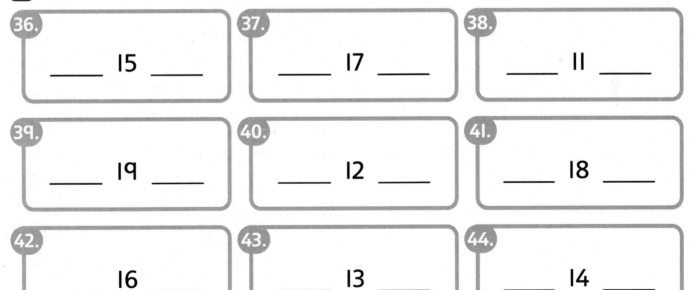

36. ___ 15 ___

37. ___ 17 ___

38. ___ 11 ___

39. ___ 19 ___

40. ___ 12 ___

41. ___ 18 ___

42. ___ 16 ___

43. ___ 13 ___

44. ___ 14 ___

☐ **BONUS:** Fill in the blanks.

45. ___ ___ ___ 14 15 16 ___ ___ ___

30. Counting Back to Subtract

☐ Subtract by counting back.

1.

5   _4_   _3_   5 − 2 = _3_

2.

4   ___   ___   ___   4 − 3 = ___

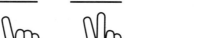

3.

6   ___ ___ ___ ___   6 − 4 = ___

4.

7   ___ ___ ___   7 − 3 = ___

5.

8   ___ ___   8 − 2 = ___

6.

5 − 3 = ___

7.

6 − 3 = ___

8.

7 − 4 = ___

31. Addition and Subtraction

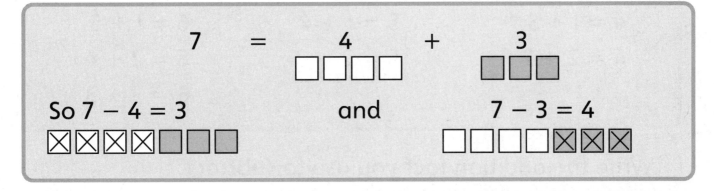

$$7 \quad = \quad 4 \quad + \quad 3$$

So $7 - 4 = 3$ and $7 - 3 = 4$

☐ Write two subtraction facts for the addition fact.

1.
$$7 = 5 + 2$$
So $\quad 7 - \underline{\;2\;} = \underline{\;5\;}$
and $\quad 7 - \underline{\;5\;} = \underline{\;2\;}$

2.
$$6 = 4 + 2$$
So $\quad 6 - \underline{\quad} = \underline{\quad}$
and $\quad 6 - \underline{\quad} = \underline{\quad}$

3.
$$8 = 5 + 3$$
So $\quad 8 - \underline{\quad} = \underline{\quad}$
and $\quad 8 - \underline{\quad} = \underline{\quad}$

4.
$$9 = 3 + 6$$
So $\quad 9 - \underline{\quad} = \underline{\quad}$
and $\quad 9 - \underline{\quad} = \underline{\quad}$

5.
$$10 = 6 + 4$$
So $\quad 10 - \underline{\quad} = \underline{\quad}$
and $\quad 10 - \underline{\quad} = \underline{\quad}$

6.
$$5 = 3 + 2$$
So $\quad 5 - \underline{\quad} = \underline{\quad}$
and $\quad 5 - \underline{\quad} = \underline{\quad}$

7.
$$9 = 2 + 7$$
So $\quad 9 - \underline{\quad} = \underline{\quad}$
and $\quad 9 - \underline{\quad} = \underline{\quad}$

8.
$$4 = 3 + 1$$
So $\quad 4 - \underline{\quad} = \underline{\quad}$
and $\quad 4 - \underline{\quad} = \underline{\quad}$

$$4 = 1 + 3 \qquad 5 = 1 + 4 \qquad 6 = 1 + 5$$
$$4 = 2 + 2 \qquad 5 = 2 + 3 \qquad 6 = 2 + 4$$
$$6 = 3 + 3$$

☐ Write the addition fact you use to subtract.

9.

$5 - 3 \mid 5 = \underline{\ 3\ } + \underline{\ 2\ }$

10.

$6 - 2 \mid 6 = \underline{\ 2\ } + \underline{\ \ \ }$

11.

$6 - 5 \mid 6 = \underline{\ 5\ } + \underline{\ \ \ }$

12.

$4 - 3 \mid 4 = \underline{\ 3\ } + \underline{\ \ \ }$

13.

$6 - 3 \mid 6 = \underline{\ \ \ } + \underline{\ \ \ }$

14.

$6 - 4 \mid 6 = \underline{\ \ \ } + \underline{\ \ \ }$

☐ Subtract by using an addition fact.

15.

$6 - 4 \mid$ $6 = \underline{\ 4\ } + \underline{\ 2\ }$

so $6 - 4 = \underline{\ 2\ }$

16.

$5 - 3 \mid$ $5 = \underline{\ 3\ } + \underline{\ \ \ }$

so $5 - 3 = \underline{\ \ \ }$

17.

$6 - 3 \mid$ $6 = \underline{\ \ \ } + \underline{\ \ \ }$

so $6 - 3 = \underline{\ \ \ }$

18.

$4 - 3 \mid$ $4 = \underline{\ \ \ } + \underline{\ \ \ }$

so $4 - 3 = \underline{\ \ \ }$

19.

$5 - 2 \mid$ $5 = \underline{\ \ \ } + \underline{\ \ \ }$

so $5 - 2 = \underline{\ \ \ }$

20.

$6 - 5 \mid$ $6 = \underline{\ \ \ } + \underline{\ \ \ }$

so $6 - 5 = \underline{\ \ \ }$

$$7 = 1 + 6 \qquad 8 = 1 + 7 \qquad 9 = 1 + 8$$
$$7 = 2 + 5 \qquad 8 = 2 + 6 \qquad 9 = 2 + 7$$
$$7 = 3 + 4 \qquad 8 = 3 + 5 \qquad 9 = 3 + 6$$
$$ \qquad 8 = 4 + 4 \qquad 9 = 4 + 5$$

☐ Subtract by using an addition fact.

21.

$7 - 2$ | $7 = \underline{\ 2\ } + \underline{\ 5\ }$
so $7 - 2 = \underline{\quad}$

22.

$7 - 3$ | $7 = \underline{\quad} + \underline{\quad}$
so $7 - 3 = \underline{\quad}$

23.

$7 - 5$ | $7 = \underline{\quad} + \underline{\quad}$
so $7 - 5 = \underline{\quad}$

24.

$7 - 4$ | $7 = \underline{\quad} + \underline{\quad}$
so $7 - 4 = \underline{\quad}$

25.

$8 - 4$ | $8 = \underline{\quad} + \underline{\quad}$
so $8 - 4 = \underline{\quad}$

26.

$8 - 3$ | $8 = \underline{\quad} + \underline{\quad}$
so $8 - 3 = \underline{\quad}$

27.

$8 - 5$ | $8 = \underline{\quad} + \underline{\quad}$
so $8 - 5 = \underline{\quad}$

28.

$9 - 4$ | $9 = \underline{\quad} + \underline{\quad}$
so $9 - 4 = \underline{\quad}$

29.

$9 - 6$ | $9 = \underline{\quad} + \underline{\quad}$
so $9 - 6 = \underline{\quad}$

30.

$9 - 7$ | $9 = \underline{\quad} + \underline{\quad}$
so $9 - 7 = \underline{\quad}$

32. Subtract to Get 10

☐ Use a chart to subtract.

1.

1	2	3	4	5	6	7	8	9	10

☒	☒	☒

13 − 3 = __10__

2.

1	2	3	4	5	6	7	8	9	10

11	12	13	14	15

15 − 5 = _____

3.

1	2	3	4	5	6	7	8	9	10

11	12	13	14

14 − 4 = _____

4.

1	2	3	4	5	6	7	8	9	10

11	12	13	14	15	16

16 − 6 = _____

5.

1	2	3	4	5	6	7	8	9	10

11	12	13	14	15	16	17	18	19

19 − 9 = _____

6.

1	2	3	4	5	6	7	8	9	10

11	12	13	14	15	16	17

17 − 7 = _____

JUMP Math Accumula

☐ Subtract.

7. 13 − 3 = ____

8. 17 − 7 = ____

9. 18 − 8 = ____

10. 12 − 2 = ____

11. 15 − 5 = ____

12. 16 − 6 = ____

13. 19 − 9 = ____

14. 14 − 4 = ____

15. 11 − 1 = ____

☐ Fill in the blank.

16. 17 − ____ = 10

17. 18 − ____ = 10

18. 11 − ____ = 10

19. 12 − ____ = 10

20. 13 − ____ = 10

21. 19 − ____ = 10

22. 15 − ____ = 10

23. 14 − ____ = 10

24. 16 − ____ = 10

☐ Find the answer.

25.

Grace has 12 apples.

She eats 2 of them.

How many are left?

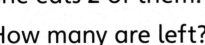

33. Subtracting from the Teens Using 10

◯ Take away ■ to get to 10.
◯ Then take away ☐ from 10.

1.

15 − 7

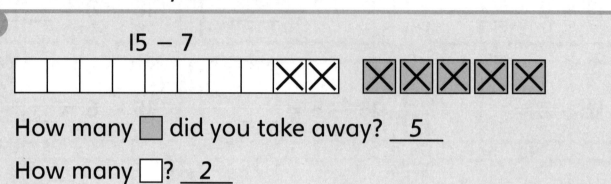

How many ■ did you take away? __5__

How many ☐? __2__

2.

14 − 6

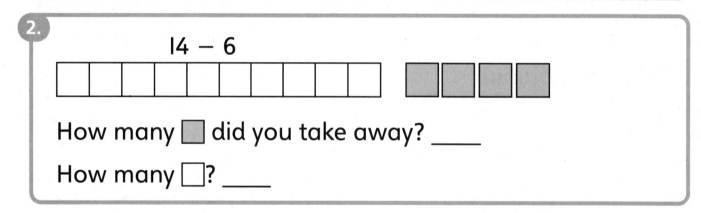

How many ■ did you take away? _____

How many ☐? _____

3.

16 − 8

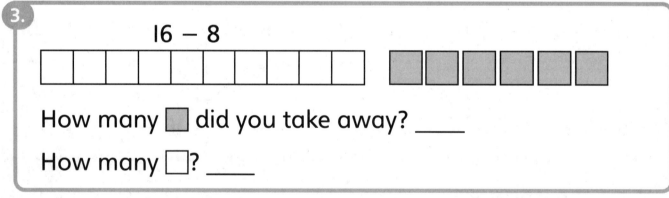

How many ■ did you take away? _____

How many ☐? _____

4.

13 − 7

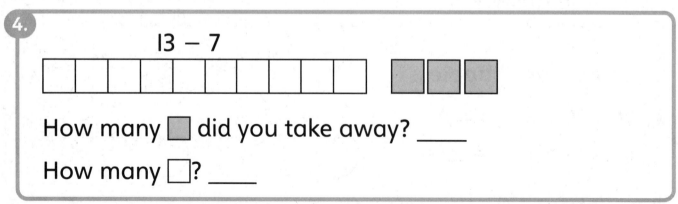

How many ■ did you take away? _____

How many ☐? _____

$$4 = 1 + 3 \qquad 5 = 1 + 4 \qquad 6 = 1 + 5$$

$$4 = 2 + 2 \qquad 5 = 2 + 3 \qquad 6 = 2 + 4$$

$$6 = 3 + 3$$

☐ How many do you take away to make 10?
☐ How many does that leave?

5.

$$12 \quad - \quad 6$$

$$12 - \underline{\;\;2\;\;} - \underline{\;\;4\;\;}$$

This makes 10.

6.

$$14 \quad - \quad 6$$

$$14 - \underline{\;\;4\;\;} - \underline{\;\;\;\;\;}$$

This makes 10.

7.

$$12 \quad - \quad 5$$

$$12 - \underline{\;\;2\;\;} - \underline{\;\;\;\;\;}$$

8.

$$14 \quad - \quad 5$$

$$14 - \underline{\;\;4\;\;} - \underline{\;\;\;\;\;}$$

9.

$$13 \quad - \quad 4$$

$$13 - \underline{\;\;3\;\;} - \underline{\;\;\;\;\;}$$

10.

$$12 \quad - \quad 4$$

$$12 - \underline{\;\;\;\;\;} - \underline{\;\;\;\;\;}$$

11.

$$15 \quad - \quad 6$$

$$15 - \underline{\;\;\;\;\;} - \underline{\;\;\;\;\;}$$

12.

$$11 \quad - \quad 6$$

$$11 - \underline{\;\;\;\;\;} - \underline{\;\;\;\;\;}$$

$$7 = 1 + 6 \qquad 8 = 1 + 7 \qquad 9 = 1 + 8$$
$$7 = 2 + 5 \qquad 8 = 2 + 6 \qquad 9 = 2 + 7$$
$$7 = 3 + 4 \qquad 8 = 3 + 5 \qquad 9 = 3 + 6$$
$$8 = 4 + 4 \qquad 9 = 4 + 5$$

 How many do you take away to make 10?

 How many does that leave?

13.
16   –   7

16 – __6__ – __1__

14.
12   –   8

12 – __2__ – _____

15.
15   –   8

15 – _____ – _____

16.
14   –   7

14 – _____ – _____

17.
15   –   9

15 – _____ – _____

18.
16   –   8

16 – _____ – _____

19.
17   –   9

17 – _____ – _____

20.
11   –   7

11 – _____ – _____

☐ Subtract by making 10.

21.

13 $-$ 5

$= 13 - \underline{\ 3\ } - \underline{\ 2\ }$

$= 10 - \underline{\ 2\ }$

$= \underline{\ 8\ }$

22.

15 $-$ 8

$= 15 - \underline{\ 5\ } - \underline{\ \ \ }$

$= 10 - \underline{\ \ \ }$

$= \underline{\ \ \ }$

23.

16 $-$ 7

$= 16 - \underline{\ \ \ } - \underline{\ \ \ }$

$= 10 - \underline{\ \ \ }$

$= \underline{\ \ \ }$

24.

12 $-$ 6

$= 12 - \underline{\ \ \ } - \underline{\ \ \ }$

$= 10 - \underline{\ \ \ }$

$= \underline{\ \ \ }$

25.

15 $-$ 7

$= 15 - \underline{\ \ \ } - \underline{\ \ \ }$

$= 10 - \underline{\ \ \ }$

$= \underline{\ \ \ }$

26.

14 $-$ 5

$= 14 - \underline{\ \ \ } - \underline{\ \ \ }$

$= 10 - \underline{\ \ \ }$

$= \underline{\ \ \ }$

27. $13 - 8$

28. $14 - 7$

29. $18 - 9$

30. $17 - 8$

31. $13 - 4$

32. $15 - 6$

33. $16 - 9$

34. $12 - 4$

34. Subtraction Word Problems

☐ Draw a picture to subtract.

1.

10 children   3 leave

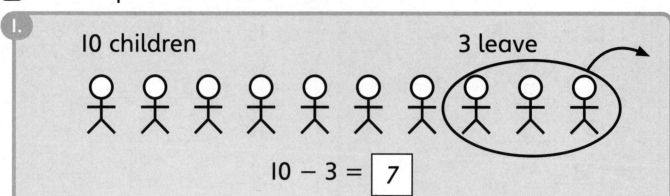

10 − 3 = ⬚ 7

2.

8 children   5 leave

8 − 5 = ⬚

3.

6 children   2 leave

6 − 2 = ⬚

4.

7 children   5 leave

7 − 5 = ⬚

☐ Draw circles to subtract.

5.

10 flies are buzzing.

A frog eats 4 of them.

⊗ ⊗ ⊗ ⊗ ◯ ◯ ◯ ◯ ◯ ◯

How many are left? __6__

6.

Bianca has 5 pencils.

She loses 2 of them.

How many does she have now? ____

7.

Carl has 8 crayons.

He gives 3 of them to Kate.

How many does Carl have left? ____

8.

Anne has 9 balloons.

8 of them pop.

How many are left? ____

☐ Draw circles to subtract.

9.

8 children play soccer.

4 leave to go down a slide.

How many are still playing soccer? _____

10.

5 birds are on a tree.

3 of them fly away.

How many birds are on the tree now? _____

11.

Roy has 8 stamps.

He uses 3 of them.

How many stamps are left? _____

12.

6 puppies are in a box.

2 climb out.

How many are in the box now? _____

35. Making 10 to Add

☐ Use the group of 10 to help you add.

1.

7   5

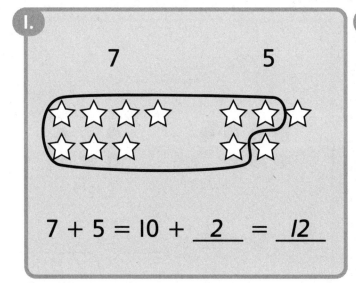

$7 + 5 = 10 + \underline{\ 2\ } = \underline{\ 12\ }$

2.

7   6

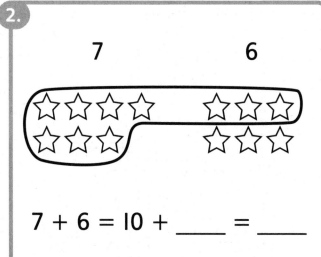

$7 + 6 = 10 + \underline{\quad} = \underline{\quad}$

3.

9   5

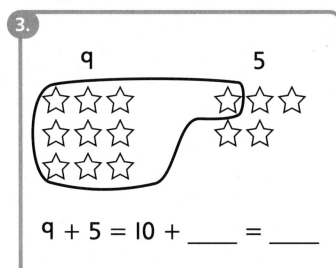

$9 + 5 = 10 + \underline{\quad} = \underline{\quad}$

4.

6   8

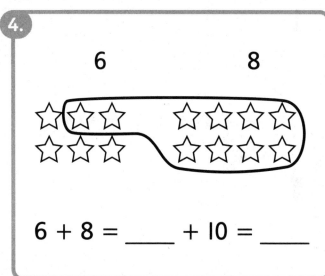

$6 + 8 = \underline{\quad} + 10 = \underline{\quad}$

5.

4   8

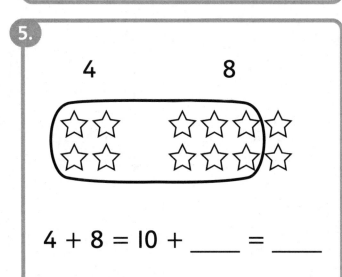

$4 + 8 = 10 + \underline{\quad} = \underline{\quad}$

6.

3   9

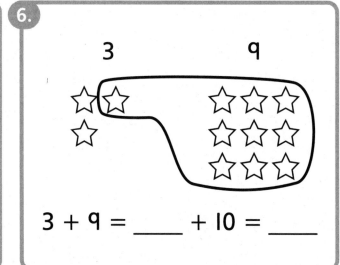

$3 + 9 = \underline{\quad} + 10 = \underline{\quad}$

☐ Circle a group of 10 dots.
☐ Use 10 to add.

7.
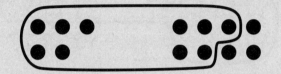

5   8

5 + 8 = 10 + __3__ = __13__

8.

7   5

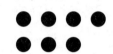

7 + 5 = 10 + ____ = ____

9.

9   3

9 + 3 = ____ + 10 = ____

10.

8   4

8 + 4 = 10 + ____ = ____

11.

6   7

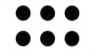

6 + 7 = 10 + ____ = ____

12.

3   8

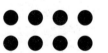

3 + 8 = ____ + 10 = ____

36. Addition Greater Than 10

☐ Underline the blocks needed to make 10.
☐ Write the number.

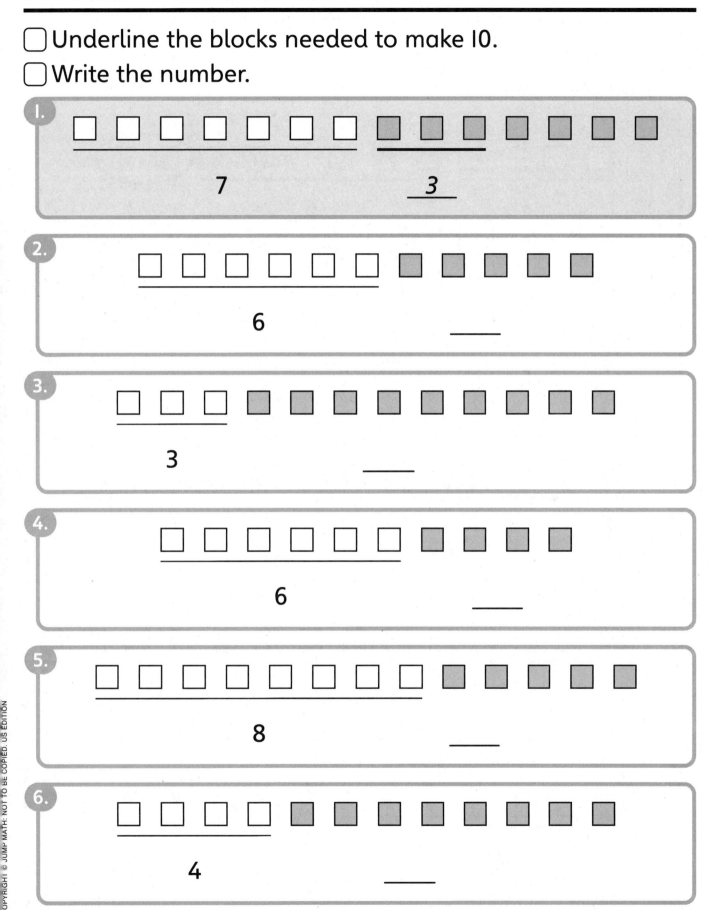

1. 7   _3_

2. 6   ____

3. 3   ____

4. 6   ____

5. 8   ____

6. 4   ____

☐ Underline the blocks needed to make 10.
☐ Circle the rest.
☐ Write the numbers.

7.

☐ ☐ ☐ ☐ ■ ■ ■ ■ ■ ■ (■ ■)

4   6   2

8.

☐ ☐ ☐ ☐ ☐ ■ ■ ■ ■ ■ ■ ■ ■

5   ____   ____

9.

☐ ☐ ☐ ☐ ☐ ☐ ☐ ☐ ■ ■ ■ ■ ■

8   ____   ____

10.

☐ ☐ ☐ ☐ ☐ ☐ ☐ ■ ■ ■ ■ ■ ■ ■ ■

7   ____   ____

11.

☐ ☐ ☐ ☐ ☐ ☐ ☐ ☐ ■ ■ ■ ■ ■ ■ ■

8   ____   ____

☐ How many blocks do you add to make 10?

☐ How many are left?

☐ Use 10 to add.

12.

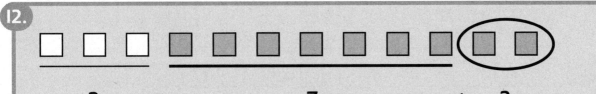

3   +   _7_   + _2_   = _12_

13.

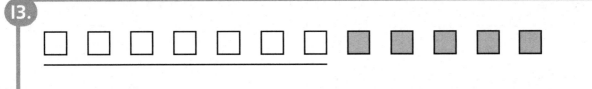

7   + ___ + ___   = ___

14.

3   +   ___   +   ___   = ___

15.

6   +   ___   + ___ = ___

16.

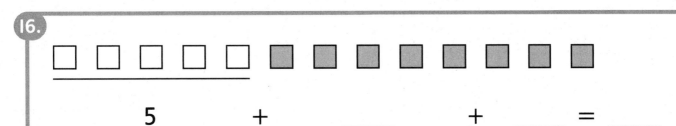

5   +   ___   + ___ = ___

37. More Addition Greater Than 10

⬜ Add the white blocks and the gray blocks.
⬜ Count all the blocks.

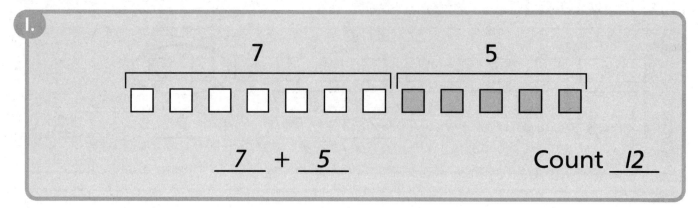

1.

7   5

_7_ + _5_   Count _12_

2.

4   q

___ + ___   Count ____

3.

4   8

___ + ___   Count ____

4.

8   6

___ + ___   Count ____

☐ Underline the blocks needed to make 10.
☐ Circle the rest.
☐ Add.

5.

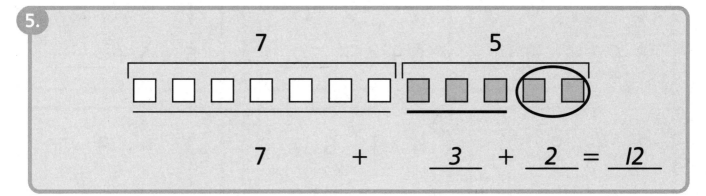

7   5

7   +   _3_ + _2_ = _12_

6.

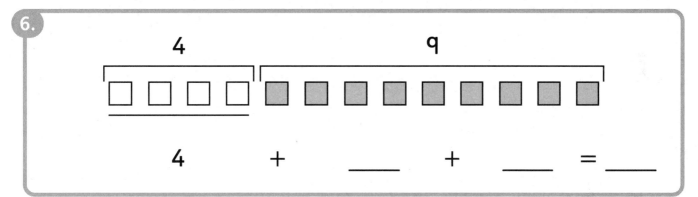

4   q

4   +   ___ + ___ = ___

7.

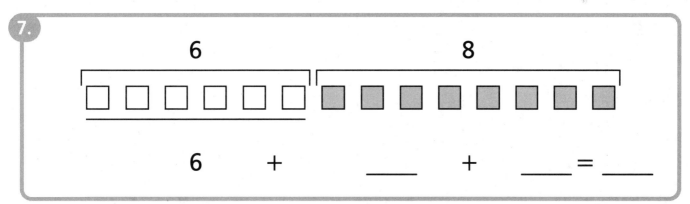

6   8

6   +   ___ + ___ = ___

8.

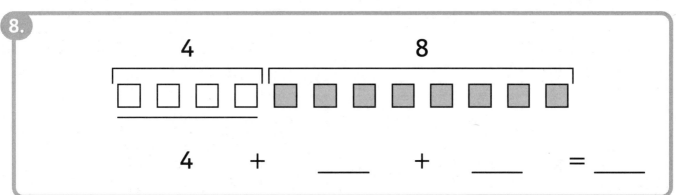

4   8

4   +   ___ + ___ = ___

☐ When you add to make 10, how many are left?

9.
8   +   5

8 + 2 + __3__

10.
6   +   8

6 + 4 + ___

11.
5   +   9

5 + 5 + ___

12.
2   +   9

2 + 8 + ___

13.
4   +   8

4 + 6 + ___

14.
3   +   9

3 + 7 + ___

15.
8   +   9

8 + 2 + ___

16.
7   +   6

7 + 3 + ___

17.
3   +   8

3 + 7 + ___

☐ Fill in the blank.

18.
5   +   7

5 + 5 + ___

19.
6   +   7

6 + 4 + ___

20.
8   +   4

8 + 2 + ___

21.
9   +   3

9 + 1 + ___

22.
2   +   9

2 + 8 + ___

23.
4   +   7

4 + 6 + ___

JUMP Math Accumula

☐ How many do you add to make 10?

☐ How many are left?

24.

8 + 3

8 + ___ + ___

25.

5 + 6

5 + ___ + ___

26.

8 + 5

8 + ___ + ___

27.

6 + 6

6 + ___ + ___

28.

3 + 9

3 + ___ + ___

29.

7 + 7

7 + ___ + ___

☐ Add using 10.

30.

7 + 9

= 7 + ___ + ___

= 10 + ___

= ___

31.

6 + 5

= 6 + ___ + ___

= 10 + ___

= ___

32.

3 + 9

= 3 + ___ + ___

= 10 + ___

= ___

33.

8 + 4

= 8 + ___ + ___

= 10 + ___

= ___

34.

6 + 9

= 6 + ___ + ___

= 10 + ___

= ___

35.

5 + 8

= 5 + ___ + ___

= 10 + ___

= ___

38. Comparing to 5

☐ Count the fingers that are up.
☐ How many more than 5?

1.

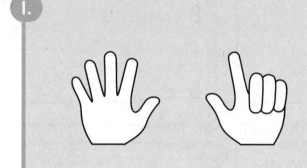

_7_ is _2_ more than 5.

2.

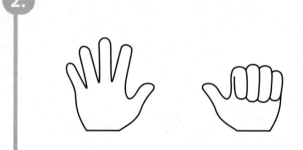

_6_ is ____ more than 5.

3.

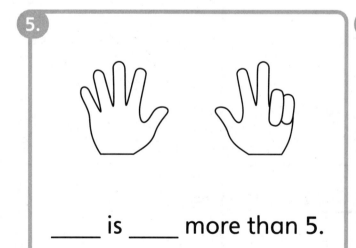

____ is ____ more than 5.

4.

____ is ____ more than 5.

5.

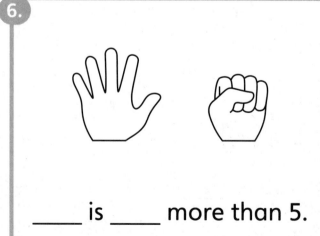

____ is ____ more than 5.

6.

____ is ____ more than 5.

☐ Count the fingers that are **not** up.
☐ How many less than 5?

7.

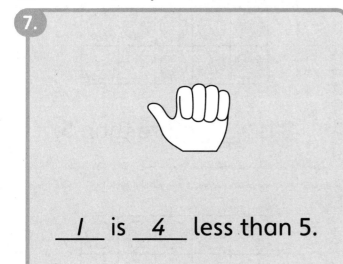

__/__ is __4__ less than 5.

8.

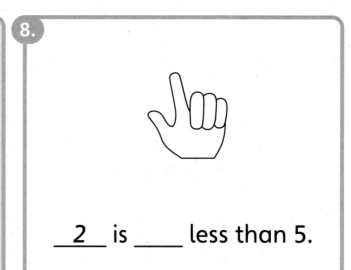

__2__ is ____ less than 5.

9.

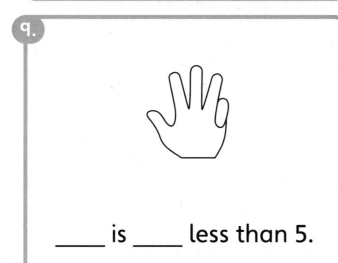

____ is ____ less than 5.

10.

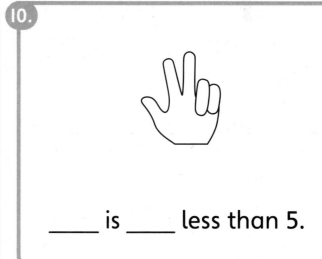

____ is ____ less than 5.

11.

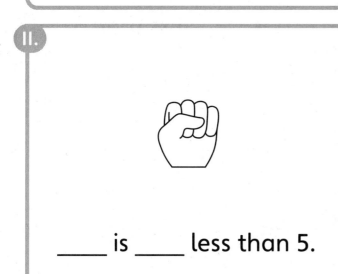

____ is ____ less than 5.

12.

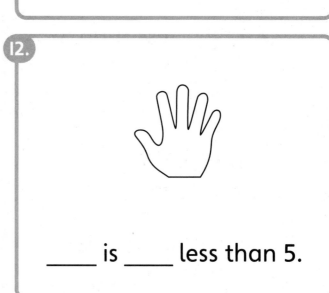

____ is ____ less than 5.

How many more than 5?

13.

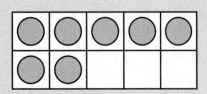

7 is __2__ more than 5.

14.

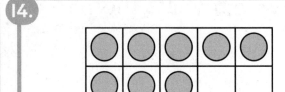

8 is _____ more than 5.

15.

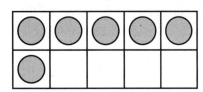

6 is _____ more than 5.

16.

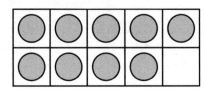

9 is _____ more than 5.

How many less than 5?

17.

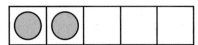

2 is _____ less than 5.

18.

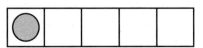

1 is _____ less than 5.

19.

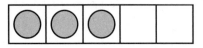

3 is _____ less than 5.

20.

4 is _____ less than 5.

☐ How many more or less than 5?

21.

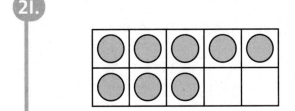

_____ is _____ more than 5.

22.

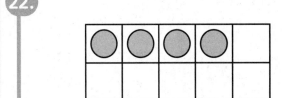

_____ is _____ less than 5.

23.

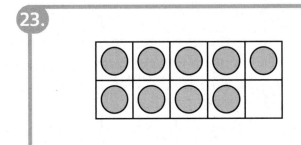

_____ is _____ more than 5.

24.

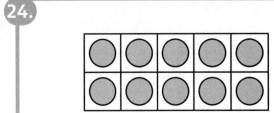

_____ is _____ more than 5.

25.

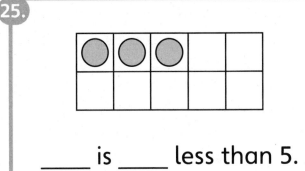

_____ is _____ less than 5.

26.

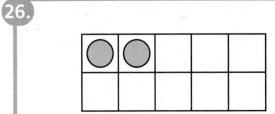

_____ is _____ less than 5.

27.

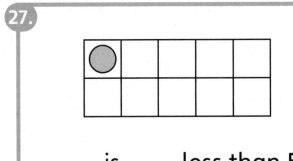

_____ is _____ less than 5.

28.

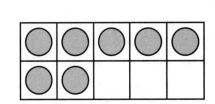

_____ is _____ more than 5.

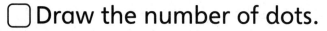
Draw the number of dots.
Fill in the blank.

29.

5 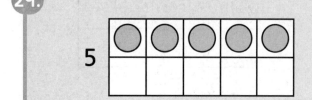   7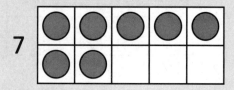

7 is __2__ more than 5.

30.

5    8

8 is ____ more than 5.

31.

5 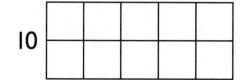   10

10 is ____ more than 5.

32.

5    6

6 is ____ more than 5.

JUMP Math Accumula

☐ How many less than 10?

1.
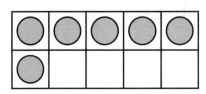

6 is _____ less than 10.

2.
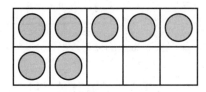

7 is _____ less than 10.

3.
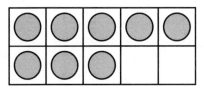

8 is _____ less than 10.

4.
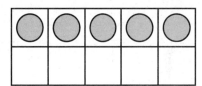

5 is _____ less than 10.

5.
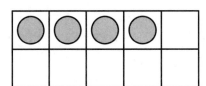

4 is _____ less than 10.

6.
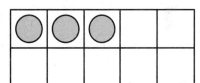

3 is _____ less than 10.

7.
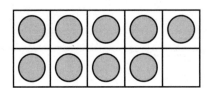

9 is _____ less than 10.

8.

1 is _____ less than 10.

1	2	3	4	5	6	7	8	9	10
11	12	13	14	15	16	17	18	19	20

☐ How many more than 10?

9.

14 is __4__ more than 10.

10.

17 is _____ more than 10.

11.

19 is _____ more than 10.

12.

15 is _____ more than 10.

13.

11 is _____ more than 10.

14.

18 is _____ more than 10.

15.

16 is _____ more than 10.

16.

12 is _____ more than 10.

17.

13 is _____ more than 10.

18. BONUS

20 is _____ 10.

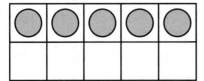 5

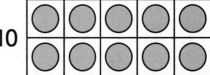 10

☐ Draw the dots.
☐ Fill in the blanks.

19.

 8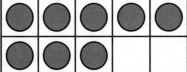

8 is __3__ more than 5.

8 is __2__ less than 10.

20.

9

9 is ____ more than 5.

9 is ____ less than 10.

21.

7

7 is ____ more than 5.

7 is ____ less than 10.

22.

6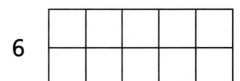

6 is ____ more than 5.

6 is ____ less than 10.

40. One More, One Less

☐ Add.

1.

$3 + 2 = 5$ ○○○ ○○

so $4 + 2 = \underline{6}$ ○○○● ○○

2.

$7 + 3 = 10$ ○○○○○○○ ○○○

so $8 + 3 = \underline{}$ ○○○○○○● ○○○

3.

$8 + 2 = 10$ ○○○○○○○ ○○

so $9 + 2 = \underline{}$ ○○○○○○○● ○○

4.

$6 + 4 = 10$ ○○○○○ ○○○○

so $6 + 5 = \underline{}$ ○○○○○ ○○○○●

5.

$4 + 1 = 5$

so $4 + 2 = \underline{}$

6.

$6 + 4 = 10$

so $7 + 4 = \underline{}$

7.

$5 + 5 = \underline{}$

so $5 + 6 = \underline{}$

8.

$3 + 2 = \underline{}$

so $3 + 3 = \underline{}$

☐ Take away I.

9.

$7 + 3 = 10$ ◯◯◯◯◯◯◯   ◯◯◯

so $7 + 2 =$ ___9___   ◯◯◯◯◯◯◯   ◯◯⊗

10.

$3 + 2 = 5$ ◯◯◯   ◯◯

so $3 + 1 =$ ____   ◯◯◯   ◯⊗

11.

$6 + 4 = 10$ ◯◯◯◯◯   ◯◯◯◯

so $5 + 4 =$ ____   ◯◯◯◯◯⊗   ◯◯◯◯

12.

$4 + 1 = 5$ ◯◯◯◯   ◯

so $4 + 0 =$ ____   ◯◯◯◯   ⊗

13.

$5 + 5 = 10$

so $4 + 5 =$ ____

14.

$2 + 3 = 5$

so $2 + 2 =$ ____

15.

$4 + 1 = 5$

so $3 + 1 =$ ____

16.

$5 + 5 = 10$

so $5 + 4 =$ ____

☐ Add I or take away I.

17.

$6 + 4 = 10$ ○○○○○   ○○○○

so $6 + 3 =$ ___   ○○○○○   ○○○⊗

18.

$6 + 4 = 10$ ○○○○○   ○○○○

so $5 + 4 =$ ___   ○○○○⊗   ○○○○

19.

$7 + 3 = 10$ ○○○○○○   ○○○

so $7 + 4 =$ ___   ○○○○○○   ○○○●

20.

$7 + 3 = 10$

so $7 + 2 =$ ___

21.

$7 + 3 = 10$

so $6 + 3 =$ ___

22.

$5 + 5 = 10$

so $5 + 6 =$ ___

23.

$5 + 5 = 10$

so $4 + 5 =$ ___

24.

$8 + 2 = 10$

so $8 + 3 =$ ___

25.

$8 + 2 =$ ___

so $7 + 2 =$ ___

41. Pictures and Number Sentences

☐ Add the circles.

1.

○ ○ ● ● ●

__2__ white + __3__ black = __5__ in total

__3__ black + __2__ white = __5__ in total

2.

● ● ● ○ ○ ○ ○ ○

____ black + ____ white = ____ in total

____ white + ____ black = ____ in total

3.

● ● ● ● ● ○ ○

____ white + ____ black = ____ in total

____ black + ____ white = ____ in total

4.

○ ○ ○ ○ ● ● ● ● ●

____ black + ____ white = ____ in total

____ white + ____ black = ____ in total

☐ Add or subtract the squares.

5.

_____ black + _____ white = _____ in total

_____ white + _____ black = _____ in total

_____ squares − _____ black = _____ white

_____ squares − _____ white = _____ black

6.

_____ black + _____ white = _____ in total

_____ white + _____ black = _____ in total

_____ squares − _____ black = _____ white

_____ squares − _____ white = _____ black

7.

_____ black + _____ white = _____ in total

_____ white + _____ black = _____ in total

_____ squares − _____ black = _____ white

_____ squares − _____ white = _____ black

☐ Write 2 addition sentences for the picture.
☐ Write 2 subtraction sentences for the picture.

8.

$4 + 1 = 5$ $1 + 4 = 5$

$5 - 4 = 1$ $5 - 1 = 4$

9.

_____   _____

_____   _____

10.

_____   _____

_____   _____

11.

_____   _____

_____   _____

Write 4 number sentences for the picture.

12.

$$\underline{\ 3\ } + \underline{\ 4\ } = \underline{\ 7\ }$$

$$\underline{\ 4\ } + \underline{\ 3\ } = \underline{\ 7\ }$$

$$\underline{\ 7\ } - \underline{\ 4\ } = \underline{\ 3\ }$$

$$\underline{\ 7\ } - \underline{\ 3\ } = \underline{\ 4\ }$$

13.

2		6
$+\ 4$		$-\ 4$
6		2

4		6
$+\ 2$		$-\ 2$
6		4

14.

$$\underline{\quad} + \underline{\quad} = \underline{\quad}$$

$$\underline{\quad} + \underline{\quad} = \underline{\quad}$$

$$\underline{\quad} - \underline{\quad} = \underline{\quad}$$

$$\underline{\quad} - \underline{\quad} = \underline{\quad}$$

15. BONUS

6		7
$+\ 1$		$-\ 1$
7		6

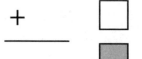

$$+ \underline{\qquad}$$

$$- \underline{\qquad}$$

16.

[picture of six squares, first shaded]

$$\underline{\hspace{6cm}}$$

$$\underline{\hspace{6cm}}$$

$$\underline{\hspace{6cm}}$$

$$\underline{\hspace{6cm}}$$

42. More Pictures and Number Sentences

☐ Add or subtract.

1.

____ dogs + ____ cats = ____ pets

____ cats + ____ dogs = ____ pets

____ pets − ____ dogs = ____ cats

____ pets − ____ cats = ____ dogs

2.

____ bunnies + ____ hamsters = ____ pets

____ hamsters + ____ bunnies = ____ pets

____ pets − ____ bunnies = ____ hamsters

____ pets − ____ hamsters = ____ bunnies

☐ Write 4 number sentences for the picture.

3.

2 + 5 = 7 _____   5 + 2 = 7 _____

7 − 5 = 2 _____   7 − 2 = 5 _____

4.

_____   _____

_____   _____

☐ Write 4 number sentences.

5.

4 cups   3 plates

_____   _____

_____   _____

6.

5 cars   2 vans

_____   _____

_____   _____

☐ How many animals?

7.
2 cats   3 dogs   4 rabbits

___ + ___ + ___ = ___

8.
2 turtles   3 frogs   1 fish

___ + ___ + ___ = ___

9.
2 goats   3 cows   3 pigs

___ + ___ + ___ = ___

10.
1 lion   5 tigers   3 bears

___ + ___ + ___ = ___

11. BONUS

3 cats   2 dogs   4 rabbits

How many animals?

___ + ___ + ___ = ___

2 rabbits hop away.

How many animals are there now?

___ − ___ = ___

43. Comparing Numbers Using Pictures

☐ Circle the **extra** 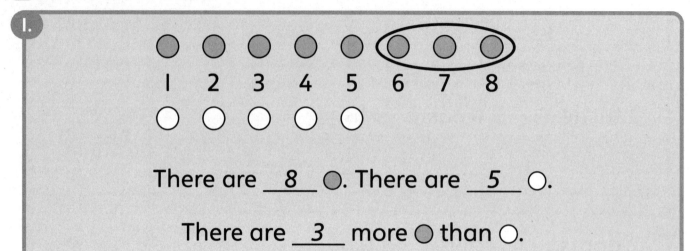 to find how many more.
☐ Fill in the blanks.

1.

There are __8__ ⬤. There are __5__ ◯.

There are __3__ more ⬤ than ◯.

2.

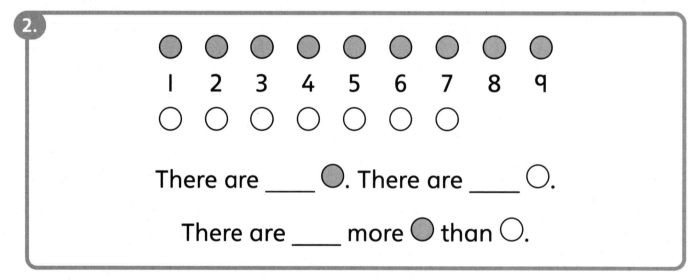

There are ____ ⬤. There are ____ ◯.

There are ____ more ⬤ than ◯.

3.

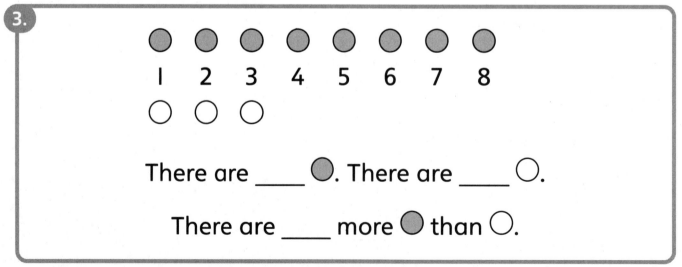

There are ____ ⬤. There are ____ ◯.

There are ____ more ⬤ than ◯.

☐ Circle the extra ○.
☐ Fill in the blanks.

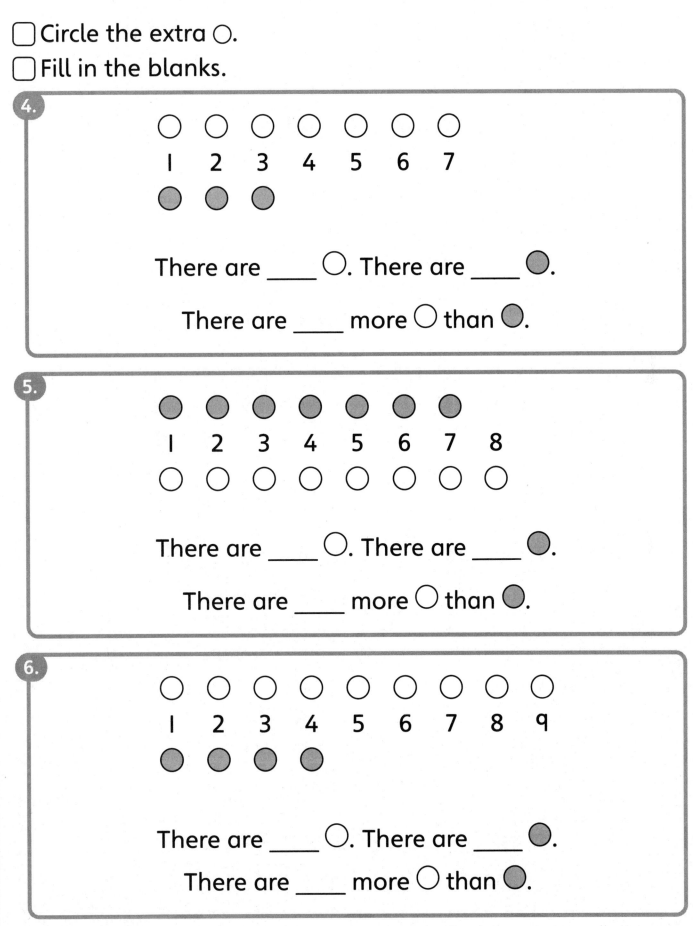

4.

○ ○ ○ ○ ○ ○ ○
1 2 3 4 5 6 7
● ● ●

There are ____ ○. There are ____ ●.

There are ____ more ○ than ●.

5.

● ● ● ● ● ● ●
1 2 3 4 5 6 7 8
○ ○ ○ ○ ○ ○ ○ ○

There are ____ ○. There are ____ ●.

There are ____ more ○ than ●.

6.

○ ○ ○ ○ ○ ○ ○ ○ ○
1 2 3 4 5 6 7 8 9
● ● ● ●

There are ____ ○. There are ____ ●.

There are ____ more ○ than ●.

☐ Circle the extra ⬤.
☐ Fill in the blanks.

7.

⬤ ⬤ ⬤ ⬤ ⬤ ⬤
1 2 3 4 5 6
○ ○ ○ ○ ○

There are ____ ⬤. There are ____ ○.
There are ____ more ⬤ than ○.

8.

⬤ ⬤ ⬤ ⬤ ⬤ ⬤ ⬤ ⬤ ⬤
1 2 3 4 5 6 7 8 9
○ ○ ○ ○ ○ ○

There are ____ ⬤. There are ____ ○.
There are ____ more ⬤ than ○.

9.

○ ○
1 2 3 4 5 6 7
⬤ ⬤ ⬤ ⬤ ⬤ ⬤ ⬤

There are ____ ⬤. There are ____ ○.
There are ____ more ⬤ than ○.

☐ Draw a picture to find the answer.
☐ Use ⬤ and ◯.

10.

5 cats ⬤ ⬤ ⬤ ⬤ ⬤

4 dogs ◯ ◯ ◯ ◯

How many more cats? ___1___

11.

4 cats

6 dogs

How many more dogs? _____

12.

6 cats

3 dogs

How many more cats? _____

13.

2 cats

7 dogs

How many more dogs? _____

44. More Addition Word Problems

☐ Draw circles to show the numbers.
☐ Write the number sentence.
☐ Fill in the answer.

1.

There are 3 cats. ● ● ●

There are 4 dogs. ○ ○ ○ ○

There are __7__ animals altogether.

$$\begin{array}{r} 3 \\ +\ 4 \\ \hline 7 \end{array}$$

2.

There are 6 yellow crayons.

There are 5 blue crayons.

There are ____ crayons in total.

$$+\ \boxed{}$$

3.

Zara has 2 big toys.

She has 8 small toys.

Zara has ____ toys in total.

$$+\ \boxed{}$$

4.

John has 7 shirts.

He has 6 sweaters.

John has ____ tops altogether.

$$+\ \boxed{}$$

☐ Draw circles to show the numbers.
☐ Write the number sentence.
☐ Fill in the answer.

5.

5 birds are in a tree.

3 birds join them.

There are ____ birds in the tree.

$$+ \begin{array}{c} \boxed{} \\ \boxed{} \\ \hline \boxed{} \end{array}$$

6.

4 frogs are in a pond.

2 frogs join them.

There are ____ frogs in the pond.

$$+ \begin{array}{c} \boxed{} \\ \boxed{} \\ \hline \boxed{} \end{array}$$

7.

6 adults are in a pool.

3 children jump in.

There are ____ people in the pool.

$$+ \begin{array}{c} \boxed{} \\ \boxed{} \\ \hline \boxed{} \end{array}$$

8.

Ken has 3 dimes.

Amy has 4 dimes.

They have ____ dimes altogether.

$$+ \begin{array}{c} \boxed{} \\ \boxed{} \\ \hline \boxed{} \end{array}$$

◻ Write the number sentence in 2 ways.

◻ Fill in the answer.

9.

Kim has 5 balls.

Ron has 3 balls.

They have ____ balls altogether.

☐ + ☐ = ☐

+

10.

Tess has 3 pens.

Ben has 2 pens.

They have ____ pens in all.

☐ + ☐ = ☐

+

11.

Raj has 4 hats.

Mary has 3 hats.

They have ____ hats in total.

☐ + ☐ = ☐

+

12.

Ava has 2 new books.

She has 3 old books.

Ava has ____ books in total.

☐ + ☐ = ☐

+

45. More Subtraction Word Problems

☐ Draw circles and cross out to subtract.
☐ Write the subtraction sentence.
☐ Fill in the answer.

1.

Jason has **8** crayons.   ⊗ ⊗ ⊗ ◯ ◯ ◯ ◯ ◯

He gives **3** to his sister.

Jason has __5__ crayons left.

$$\begin{array}{r} 8 \\ -\ 3 \\ \hline 5 \end{array}$$

2.

Helen has **4** pencils.

She loses **1** of them.

Helen has ____ pencils left.

$$\begin{array}{r} \square \\ -\ \square \\ \hline \square \end{array}$$

3.

Lily has **6** marbles.

She gives **2** to Alex.

Lily has ____ marbles left.

$$\begin{array}{r} \square \\ -\ \square \\ \hline \square \end{array}$$

4.

Sal has **5** toy cars.

His teacher takes **3** of them.

Now Sal has ____ toy cars.

$$\begin{array}{r} \square \\ -\ \square \\ \hline \square \end{array}$$

☐ Draw circles and cross out to subtract.
☐ Write the subtraction sentence.
☐ Fill in the answer.

5.

5 rabbits are on the grass.

2 of them hop away.

There are ____ rabbits on the grass.

$$\begin{array}{r} \square \\ -\ \square \\ \hline \square \end{array}$$

6.

6 frogs are on a log.

4 frogs hop off.

Now ____ frogs are on the log.

$$\begin{array}{r} \square \\ -\ \square \\ \hline \square \end{array}$$

7.

6 children play tag.

3 go home.

Now ____ children are playing tag.

$$\begin{array}{r} \square \\ -\ \square \\ \hline \square \end{array}$$

8.

Clara has 5 grapes.

She eats 3 of them.

Clara has ____ grapes left.

$$\begin{array}{r} \square \\ -\ \square \\ \hline \square \end{array}$$

JUMP Math Accumula

☐ Write the number sentence in 2 ways.

☐ Fill in the answer.

9.

Fred has 5 crayons.

He uses up 4 of them.

Now Fred has ____ crayon.

☐ − ☐ = ☐

☐
− ☐
_____
☐

10.

Rani has 4 crackers.

She eats 1 cracker.

Rani has ____ crackers left.

☐ − ☐ = ☐

☐
− ☐
_____
☐

11.

5 bears are in a cave.

3 bears leave.

There are ____ bears in the cave.

☐ − ☐ = ☐

☐
− ☐
_____
☐

12.

6 kites fly in the sky.

4 of them fall down.

There are ____ kites flying.

☐ − ☐ = ☐

☐
− ☐
_____
☐

46. Addition and Subtraction Word Problems

☐ Draw a picture to show the numbers.

☐ Write the number sentence.
Remember to write the + sign.

☐ Fill in the answer.

1.

There are 3 cats. ○ ○ ○

There are 4 dogs. ○ ○ ○ ○

There are ____ animals.

$$\begin{array}{r} 3 \\ + 4 \\ \hline 7 \end{array}$$

2.

4 birds are in a tree.

3 birds are on the ground.

There are ____ birds in total.

3.

Kim has 2 balls.

Tom has 4 balls.

They have ____ balls in total.

4.

4 books are on a table.

5 books are on a shelf.

There are ____ books in total.

☐ Draw a picture to show the numbers.
☐ Write the number sentence.
  Remember to write the − sign.
☐ Fill in the answer.

5.

Don has 5 apples.

He gives Hanna 3 apples.

Now Don has ____ apples.

☐
☐
——
☐

6.

Mandy has 6 grapes.

She eats 4 grapes.

Mandy has ____ grapes left.

☐
☐
——
☐

7.

5 rabbits are on the grass.

2 of them hop away.

Now ____ rabbits are on the grass.

☐
☐
——
☐

8.

5 cars are on the street.

3 of them drive away.

There are ____ cars on the street.

☐
☐
——
☐

☐ Draw a picture to show the numbers.
☐ Write the number sentence. Include the + or − sign.
☐ Fill in the answer.

9.

Jen has 5 balls.

Mark has 3 balls.

They have ____ balls in total.

10.

Ben has 4 balls.

He gives 3 balls away.

Ben has ____ balls left.

11.

Emma has 3 balls.

She loses 2 of them.

She has ____ ball left.

12.

Kathy has 5 balls.

Sam has 1 ball.

They have ____ balls altogether.

JUMP Math Accumula

☐ Draw a picture to show the numbers.
☐ Write a number sentence.
☐ Fill in the answer.

13.

4 cats are in a basket.

3 cats climb in.

There are ____ cats in the basket.

14.

6 cats are in a basket.

4 cats climb out.

There are ____ cats in the basket.

15.

A dog has 3 treats.

He eats 1 treat.

The dog has ____ treats left.

16.

6 dogs are in the park.

4 dogs join them.

There are ____ dogs in the park.

47. Counting to 100

☐ Shade the numbers as you count them.

1.

20 to 29

11	12	13	14	15	16	17	18	19	20
21	22	23	24	25	26	27	28	29	30

2.

30 to 39

21	22	23	24	25	26	27	28	29	30
31	32	33	34	35	36	37	38	39	40

3.

40 to 49

31	32	33	34	35	36	37	38	39	40
41	42	43	44	45	46	47	48	49	50

4.

50 to 59

41	42	43	44	45	46	47	48	49	50
51	52	53	54	55	56	57	58	59	60

61	62	63	64	65	66	67	68	69	70
71	72	73	74	75	76	77	78	79	80
81	82	83	84	85	86	87	88	89	90
91	92	93	94	95	96	97	98	99	100

☐ Use the chart to fill in the blanks.

5.

61, 62, __6__, __6__, __6__, 66

71, __7__, __7__, __7__, __7__, 76

81, _____, _____, _____, _____, 86

91, _____, _____, _____, 95, _____

☐ Fill in the blanks.

6.

54, 55, _____, _____, _____, _____

91, 92, _____, _____, _____, _____

80, 81, _____, _____, _____, _____

7.

Kim counts from 30 to 37.
She writes 30, 31, 32, 33, 84, 35, 36, 37.
Explain her mistake.

Count all the letters.

☐ Write the new total after each word.

☐ Check with a partner. Correct any mistakes.

8.

| 6 | 8 | | 17 |

Autumn   is   sometimes

☐   ☐   ☐

called   fall   because

☐   ☐   47

the   leaves   fall

☐   ☐   ☐

from   many   trees.

63   ☐   ☐

The   leaves   can

☐   ☐   ☐

turn   red,   brown,

☐   ☐   ☐

yellow,   or   orange.

48. Numbers Before and After

☐ Shade the numbers.
☐ Circle the numbers as you shade them.

1.

① ⑤ 8 9 10 11 12 14 15 18 20
21 23 25 28 29 30 31 35 38 40

1	2	3	4	5	6	7	8	9	10
11	12	13	14	15	16	17	18	19	20
21	22	23	24	25	26	27	28	29	30
31	32	33	34	35	36	37	38	39	40

2.

72 73 74 77 79 83
87 88 89 93 97 99

71	72	73	74	75	76	77	78	79	80
81	82	83	84	85	86	87	88	89	90
91	92	93	94	95	96	97	98	99	100

☐ Write the letters you made.

3.

____ ____ ____ ____

☐ Circle the number on the chart.
☐ Write what comes **after**.
☐ Write what comes **before**.

1	2	3	4	5	6	7	8	9	10
11	12	13	14	15	16	17	18	19	20
21	22	23	24	(25)	26	27	28	29	30
31	32	33	34	35	36	37	38	39	40
41	42	43	44	45	46	47	48	49	50

4.
__24__   25   __26__

5.
____   8   ____

6.
____   37   ____

7.
____   21   ____

8.
____   40   ____

9.
____   19   ____

10.
____   44   ____

11.
____   11   ____

☐ Fill in the missing numbers.

12.

33	34	35		37
43	44	45	46	47
53	54	55	56	57

13.

11	12	13	14
21	22	23	24
31		33	34

14.

21	22	23
31	32	33
41	42	
51	52	53

15.

64	65	66
	75	76
84	85	86
94	95	

16.

48	49
58	59
	69
78	79

17. BONUS

16	17	18	19	20
26	27	28	29	30
36		38	39	40
46	47	48	49	
56	57	58	59	60

18. BONUS

32		34	35	
42	43	44		46
	53	54	55	56
62	63	64	65	
72	73		75	76

1	2	3	4	5	6	7	8	9	10
11	12	13	14	15	16	17	18	19	20
21	22	23	24	25	26	27	28	29	30

20 is 2 tens blocks

☐ Use tens blocks to find the answer.

1	2	3	4	5	6	7	8	9	10
11	12	13	14	15	16	17	18	19	20
21	22	23	24	25	26	27	28	29	30
31	32	33	34	35	36	37	38	39	40
41	42	43	44	45	46	47	48	49	50

1. 30 is _____ tens blocks.

2. 40 is _____ tens blocks.

3. 50 is _____ tens blocks.

4. 10 is _____ tens block.

☐ Now answer without using blocks.

5. 60 is _____ tens blocks.

6. 70 is _____ tens blocks.

⬚ Fill in the blanks.

7.

_2_ tens blocks   =   _20_ ones blocks

8.

_____ tens blocks   =   _____ ones blocks

9.

_____ tens blocks   =   _____ ones blocks

10.

5 tens blocks   =   _____ ones blocks

11.

6 tens blocks   =   _____ ones blocks

12.

7 tens blocks   =   _____ ones blocks

☐ Fill in the blanks.

13.

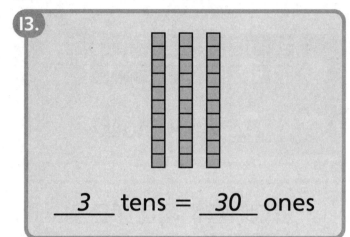

___3___ tens = ___30___ ones

14.

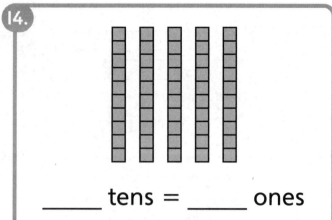

_____ tens = _____ ones

15.

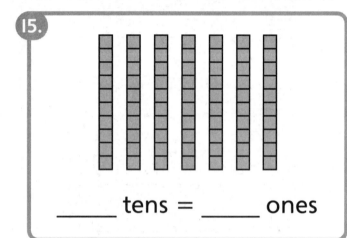

_____ tens = _____ ones

16.

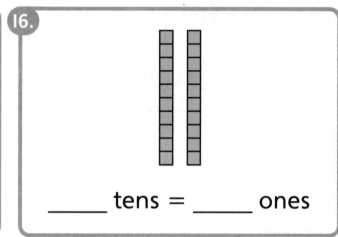

_____ tens = _____ ones

17.

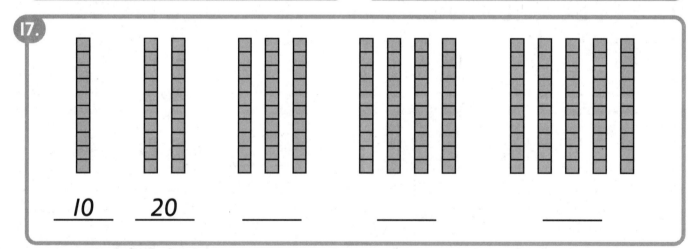

___10___   ___20___   _____   _____   _____

☐ Count by tens.

18.

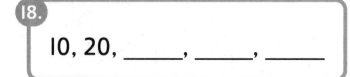

10, 20, _____, _____, _____

19.

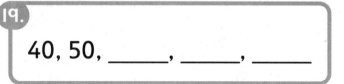

40, 50, _____, _____, _____

JUMP Math Accumula

50. Counting Groups of 10

☐ Count how many. Use groups of 10.

1.

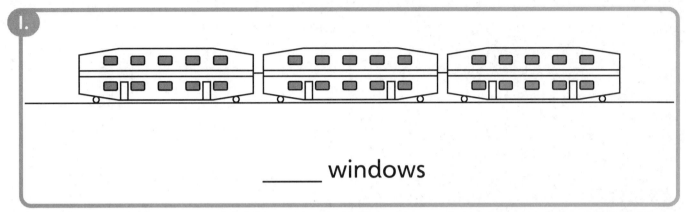

_____ windows

2.

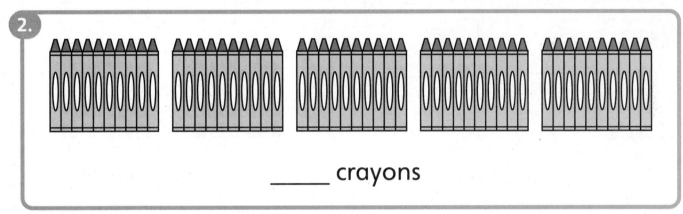

_____ crayons

3.

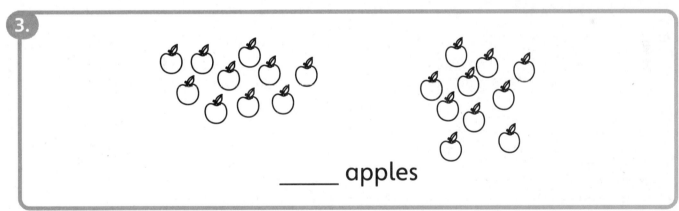

_____ apples

4.

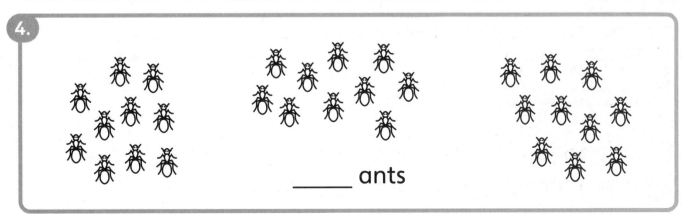

_____ ants

☐ Circle groups of 10.
☐ Write the number of ones blocks.

5.

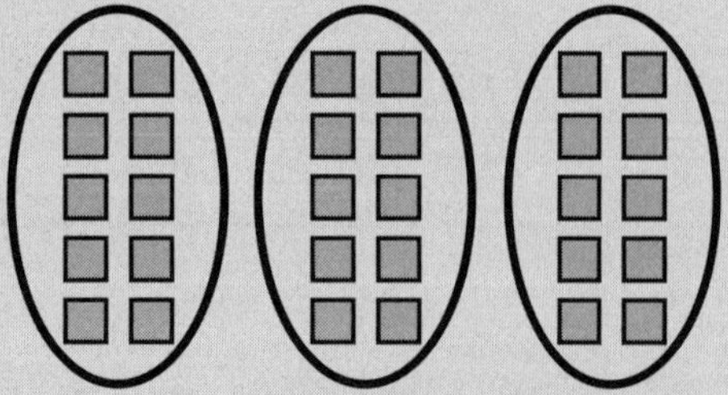

_30_ ones blocks

6.

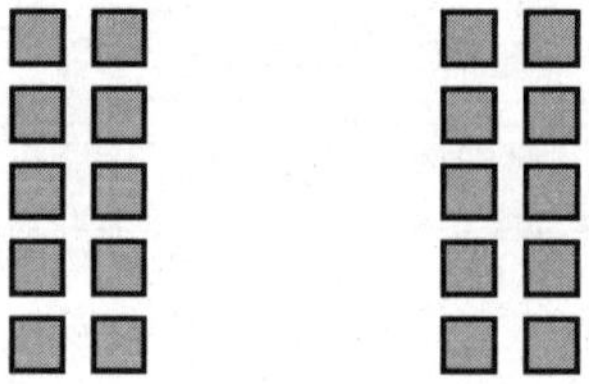

_____ ones blocks

7.

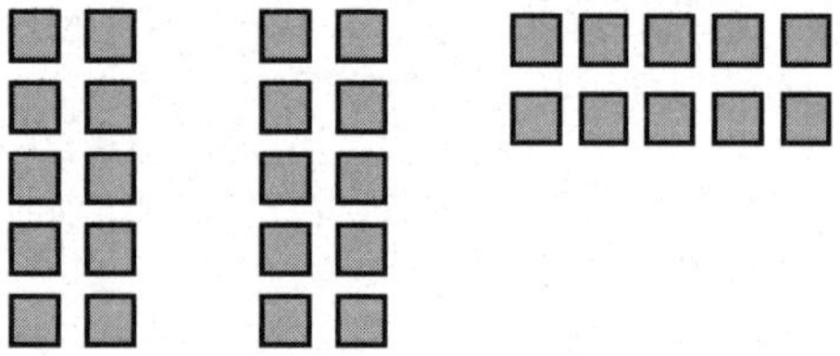

_____ ones blocks

8.

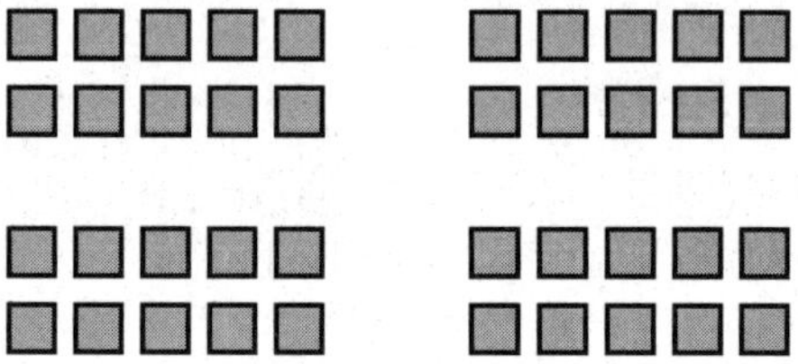

_____ ones blocks

9.

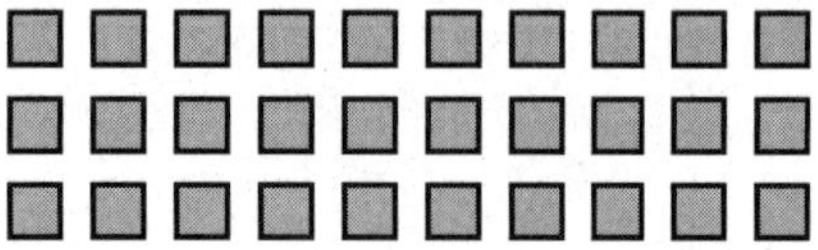

_____ ones blocks

10.

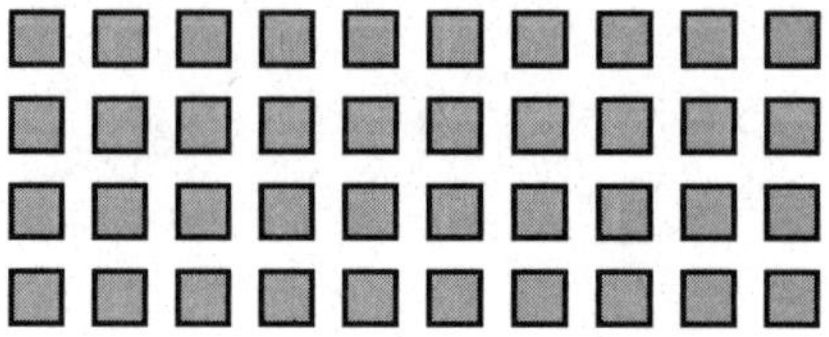

_____ ones blocks

11.

Jon says the picture shows 20 dots. Explain his mistake.

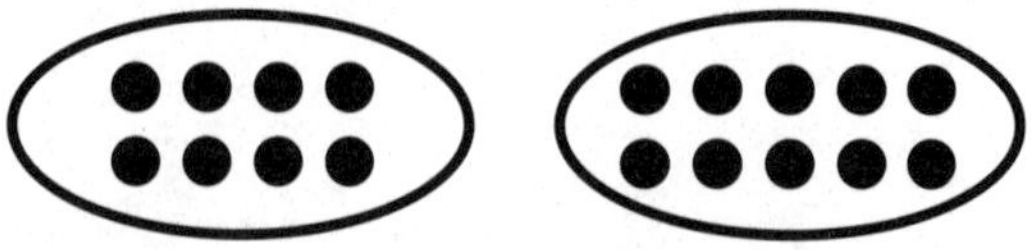

12.

Sharon puts 10 pennies in her piggy bank each day. How many pennies does she have after 4 days?

51. Tens and Ones Digits

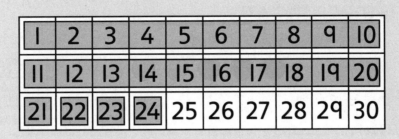

1	2	3	4	5	6	7	8	9	10
11	12	13	14	15	16	17	18	19	20
21	22	23	24	25	26	27	28	29	30

24 is 2 tens and 4 ones.

☐ Use the chart to fill in the blanks.

1	2	3	4	5	6	7	8	9	10
11	12	13	14	15	16	17	18	19	20
21	22	23	24	25	26	27	28	29	30
31	32	33	34	35	36	37	38	39	40

1. 28 is _____ tens and _____ ones.

2. 35 is _____ tens and _____ ones.

3. 27 is _____ tens and _____ ones.

4. 30 is _____ tens and _____ ones.

☐ Fill in the chart.
☐ Write the number shown.

5.

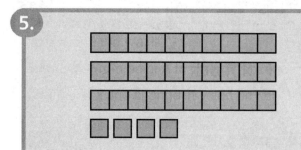

Tens	Ones
3	4

number = __34__

6.

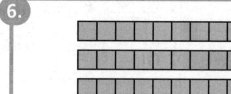
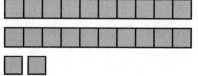

Tens	Ones

number = _____

7.

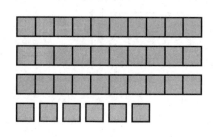

Tens	Ones

number = _____

8.

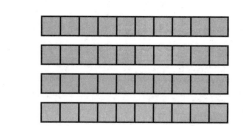

Tens	Ones

number = _____

☐ Show each number using blocks.

9.

| 50 | 43 | 37 | 19 | 32 |

JUMP Math Accumula

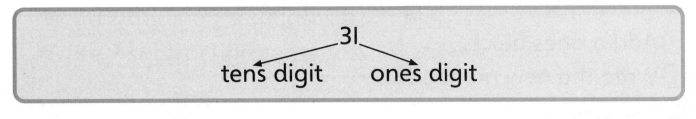

31
tens digit ↖ ↗ ones digit

☐ Circle the digit.

10. ③ 2
tens digit

11. 1 ⑦
ones digit

12. 8 1
tens digit

13. 7 5
tens digit

14. 6 3
ones digit

15. 5 2
ones digit

16. 9 8
tens digit

17. 6 6
ones digit

18. 2 3
tens digit

☐ Write the number of ones or tens.

19.

The 3 in 37 means ____3 tens____ .

The 6 in 46 means ____6 ones____ .

The 2 in 92 means _____ .

The 3 in 35 means _____ .

20. How many ones are in 2 tens blocks?

21. Don uses 3 tens blocks to show a number.
What number does he make?

52. Tens and Ones (Advanced)

☐ Add a ones block.
☐ Write the new number.

1.

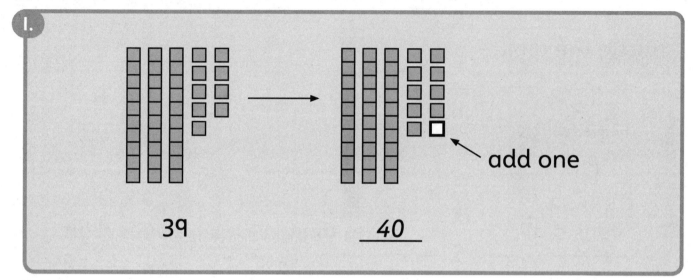

39   _40_

2.

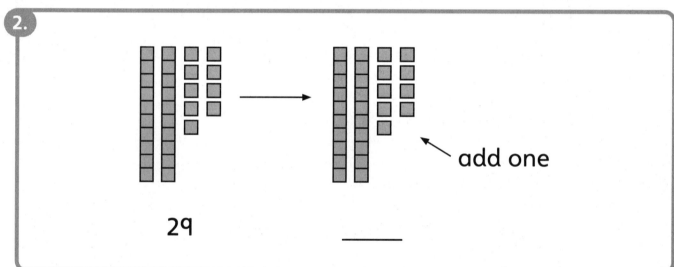

29   _____

☐ Fill in the missing number.

3.
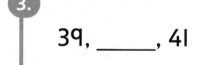
39, _____, 41

4.
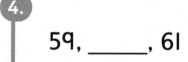
59, _____, 61

5.
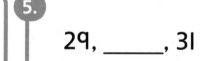
29, _____, 31

6.
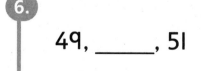
49, _____, 51

7.
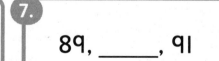
89, _____, 91

8.
69, _____, 71

☐ How many ones in all?

9.

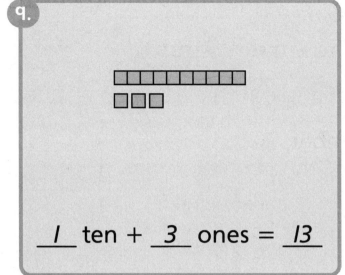

__1__ ten + __3__ ones = __13__

10.

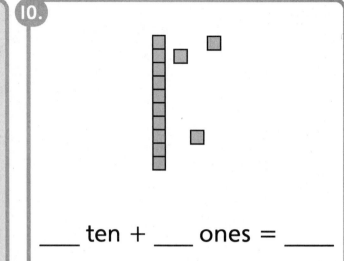

___ ten + ___ ones = ____

11.

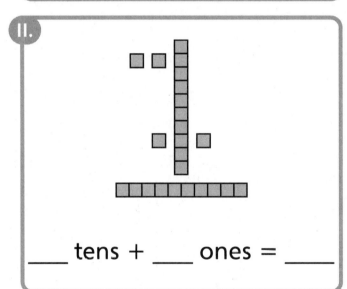

___ tens + ___ ones = ____

12.

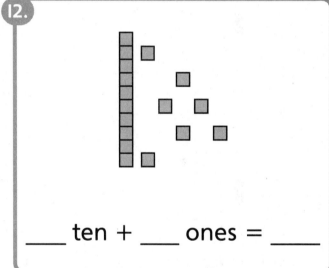

___ ten + ___ ones = ____

13.

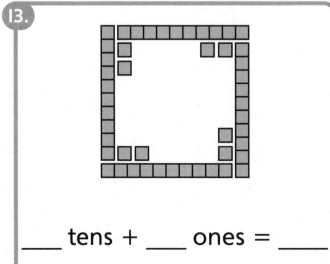

___ tens + ___ ones = ____

14.

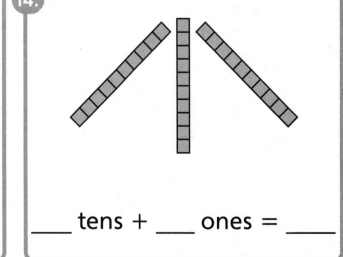

___ tens + ___ ones = ____

You can draw a line | for ▯ You can draw a dot • for ▫

◻ Draw | and • to show the number.

15.

32

16.

24

17.

43

◻ Write the number.

18.

____

19.

____

20.

____

21. BONUS

____

22. BONUS

____

53. Comparing Numbers Up to 50

☐ Use base ten blocks to show each number.
☐ Circle the **larger** number.

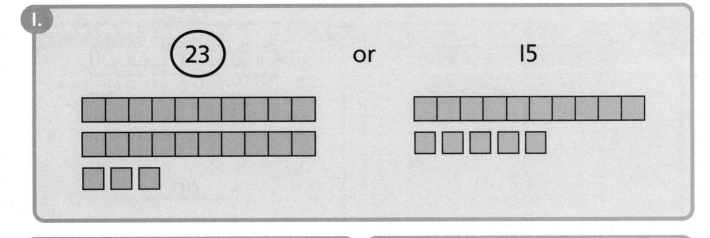

1. ⟨23⟩   or   15

2. 26   or   30

3. 40   or   45

4. 21   or   17

5. 7   or   11

6. 30   or   28

7. 26   or   29

8. 32   or   36

9. 35   or   41

10. 42   or   24

11. 13   or   31

12. 64   or   46

13. 71   or   69

☐ Can you shade 25? Write **yes** or **no**.
☐ Write the number shown.
☐ Is the number **greater** or **less** than 25?

14.

yes

_32_ is _greater_ than 25.

15.

_no_

____ is _____ than 25.

16.

_____

____ is _____ than 25.

17.

_____

____ is _____ than 25.

18.

_____

____ is _____ than 25.

19.

_____

____ is _____ than 25.

54. Comparing Numbers Up to 100

☐ Circle the largest number.

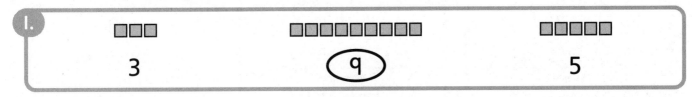

1. 3 （9） 5

2. 13 19 15

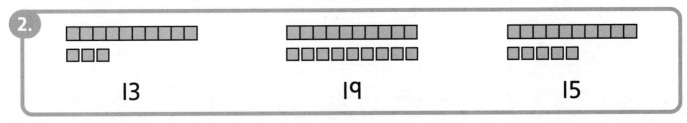

3. 23 29 25

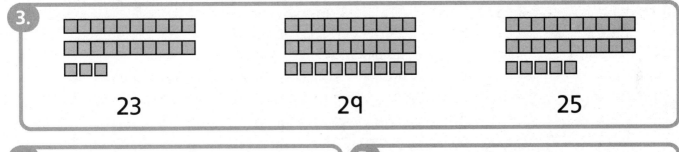

4. 43 49 45   5. 73 75 79

☐ Write the numbers in order from smallest to largest.

6. 4   7   6

   4 ____ ____

7. 34   37   36

   ____ ____ ____

8. 49   43   44

   ____ ____ ____

9. 82   80   85

   ____ ____ ____

10. BONUS

Circle the two numbers that are not in order.

51   54   55   58   57   59

☐ Circle the largest number.

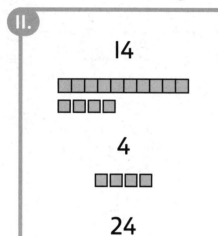

11.

14

4

24

12.

16

6

26

13.

13

3

23

14.

15

25

5

15.

34   74   54

16.

29   19   89

☐ Write the numbers in order from smallest to largest.

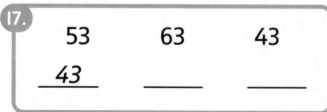

17.

53   63   43

43   _____   _____

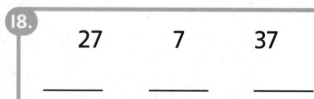

18.

27   7   37

_____   _____   _____

19. BONUS

Circle the two numbers that are not in order.

24   34   44   84   74   94

☐ Circle the larger number.

20.

☐☐☐☐☐☐☐☐☐☐   ☐☐☐☐☐☐☐☐☐
10   9

21.

☐☐☐☐☐☐☐☐☐☐
☐☐☐☐☐☐☐☐☐☐
20

☐☐☐☐☐☐☐☐☐☐
☐☐☐☐☐☐☐☐☐
19

22. 30   29

23. 49   50

24. 80   79

25. 39   40

26. 60   59

27. 90   89

28.

☐☐☐☐☐☐☐☐☐☐
☐☐☐☐☐
15

☐☐☐☐☐☐☐☐☐☐
☐☐☐☐☐☐☐☐☐☐
20

29.

☐☐☐☐☐☐☐☐☐☐
☐☐☐☐☐☐☐☐☐☐
☐☐☐☐☐☐☐☐☐☐
30

☐☐☐☐☐☐☐☐☐☐
☐☐☐☐☐☐☐☐☐☐
☐☐☐☐☐☐
26

30. 47   50

31. 60   53

32. 80   90

55. The Hundreds Chart

☐ Color all the numbers with ones digit 4 blue.

☐ Color all the numbers with tens digit 3 yellow.

1.

1	2	3	4	5	6	7	8	9	10
11	12	13	14	15	16	17	18	19	20
21	22	23	24	25	26	27	28	29	30
31	32	33	34	35	36	37	38	39	40
41	42	43	44	45	46	47	48	49	50
51	52	53	54	55	56	57	58	59	60
61	62	63	64	65	66	67	68	69	70
71	72	73	74	75	76	77	78	79	80
81	82	83	84	85	86	87	88	89	90
91	92	93	94	95	96	97	98	99	100

☐ Use the chart to answer the questions.

2.

What color is 30? _____

3.

What color is 34? _____

☐ Color all the numbers with tens digit 7 red.

☐ Color all the numbers with ones digit 2 blue.

4.

1	2	3	4	5	6	7	8	9	10
11	12	13	14	15	16	17	18	19	20
21	22	23	24	25	26	27	28	29	30
31	32	33	34	35	36	37	38	39	40
41	42	43	44	45	46	47	48	49	50
51	52	53	54	55	56	57	58	59	60
61	62	63	64	65	66	67	68	69	70
71	72	73	74	75	76	77	78	79	80
81	82	83	84	85	86	87	88	89	90
91	92	93	94	95	96	97	98	99	100

☐ Use the chart to answer the questions.

5.

What color is 22? _____

6.

What number is red and blue? _____

$\uparrow$ up	$\downarrow$ down	right $\longrightarrow$	left $\longleftarrow$

☐ Draw an arrow to show the direction you move on a hundreds chart.

7.

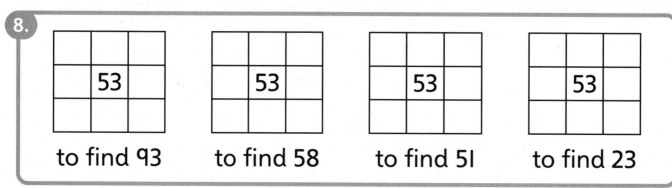

to find 41   to find 27   to find 49   to find 97

8.

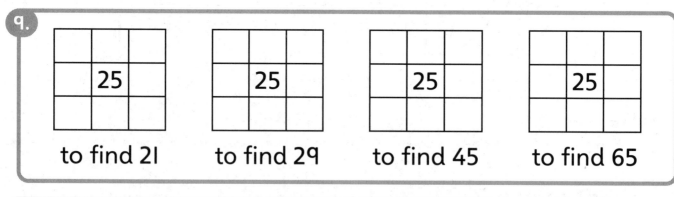

to find 93   to find 58   to find 51   to find 23

9.

to find 21   to find 29   to find 45   to find 65

10.

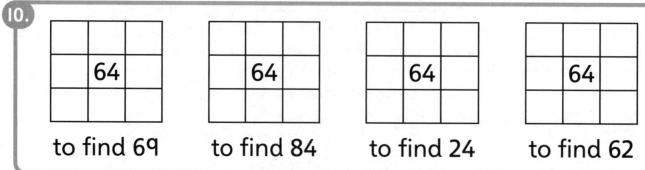

to find 69   to find 84   to find 24   to find 62

56. Ordering Numbers Up to 100

⬜ Write the numbers in order from smallest to largest.

1.

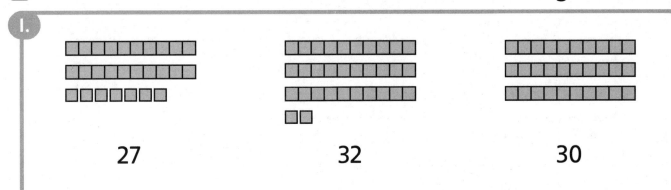

27   32   30

_____ _____ _____

2.

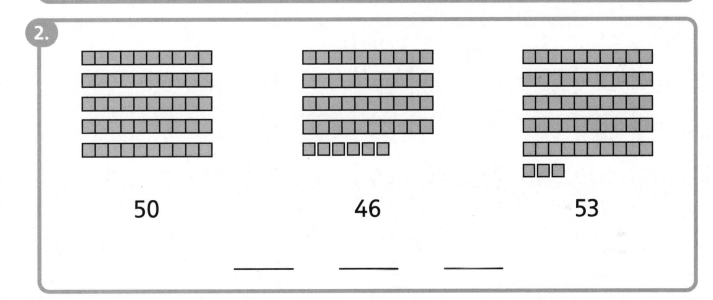

50   46   53

_____ _____ _____

3.

57   61   50

_____ _____ _____

4.

23   18   20

_____ _____ _____

Zara tries to write the numbers from smallest to largest.

⬜ Circle Zara's mistake.

5.

23 25 34 30 41

6.

54 73 68 75 80

☐ Write the shaded numbers in order.

7.

31	32	33	34	35	36	37	38	39	40
41	42	43	44	45	46	47	48	49	50
51	52	53	54	55	56	57	58	59	60

33 ___ ___ ___ ___ ___ ___

8.

51	52	53	54	55	56	57	58	59	60
61	62	63	64	65	66	67	68	69	70
71	72	73	74	75	76	77	78	79	80

___ ___ ___ ___ ___ ___ ___ ___

9.

71	72	73	74	75	76	77	78	79	80
81	82	83	84	85	86	87	88	89	90
91	92	93	94	95	96	97	98	99	100

___ ___ ___ ___ ___ ___ ___ ___

☐ Look at a meter stick to check your answers.

☐ Shade the numbers.
☐ Circle the numbers as you shade them.
☐ Write the numbers in order.

10.

(41)   38   22   35   29   40   47

21	22	23	24	25	26	27	28	29	30
31	32	33	34	35	36	37	38	39	40
41	42	43	44	45	46	47	48	49	50

___ ___ ___ ___ ___ ___ ___

11.

59   42   63   56   45   50   61

41	42	43	44	45	46	47	48	49	50
51	52	53	54	55	56	57	58	59	60
61	62	63	64	65	66	67	68	69	70

___ ___ ___ ___ ___ ___ ___

57. Number Sentences (I)

Some balls are hidden in a box.

The same number of balls is on each table.

◯ Draw the hidden balls.

◯ How many balls are hidden?

1.

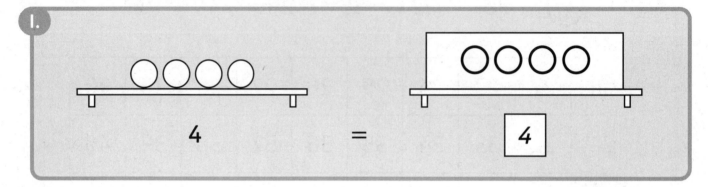

4   =   4

2.

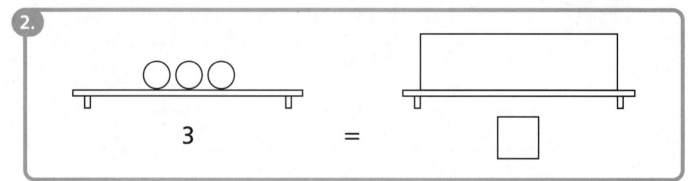

3   =

3.

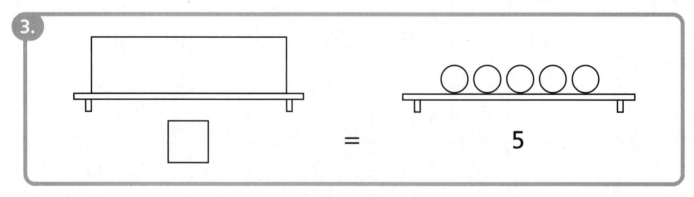

          =   5

4.

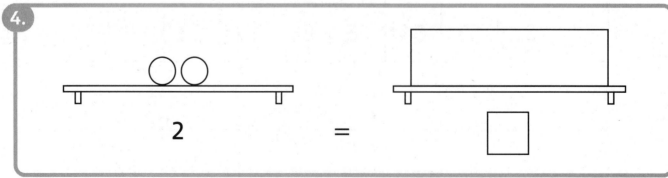

2   =

☐ Draw the hidden balls.
☐ Write the number of balls that are hidden.

5.

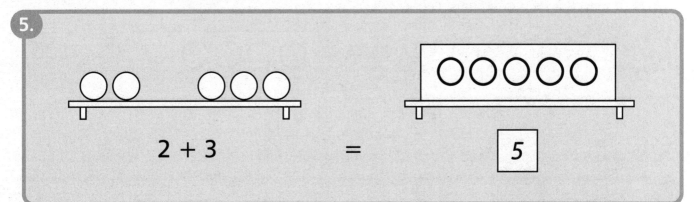

$2 + 3$ $=$ 5

6.

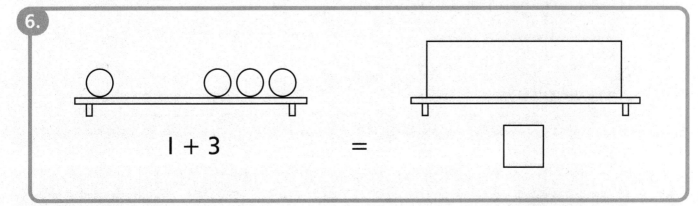

$1 + 3$ $=$

7.

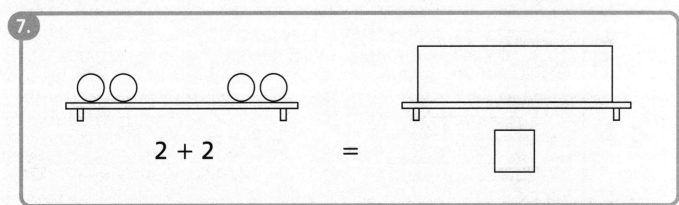

$2 + 2$ $=$

8.

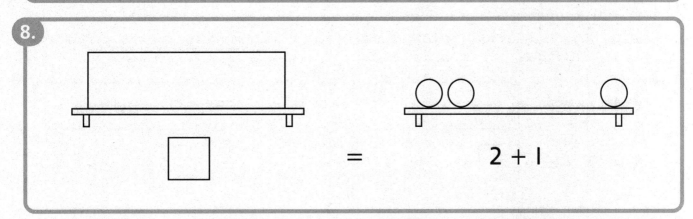

$=$ $2 + 1$

☐ Draw the hidden balls.
☐ Write the number of balls that are hidden.

9.

○○○ + ○ = [○○○○]

3 + 1 = [4]

10.

○○ + ○○ = [　　　　]

2 + 2 = [　]

11.

1 + 4 = [○○○○○]

1 + 4 = [　]

12.

2 + 1 = [　　　]

2 + 1 = [　]

13.

1 + 3 = [　　　]

1 + 3 = [　]

14.

3 + 2 = [　　　]

3 + 2 = [　]

15.

1 + 1 = [　　　]

1 + 1 = [　]

58. Number Sentences (2)

☐ Draw the hidden balls.
☐ Write the number of balls that are hidden.

1.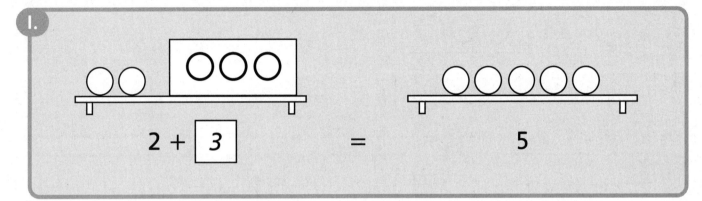

$$2 + \boxed{3} \qquad = \qquad 5$$

2.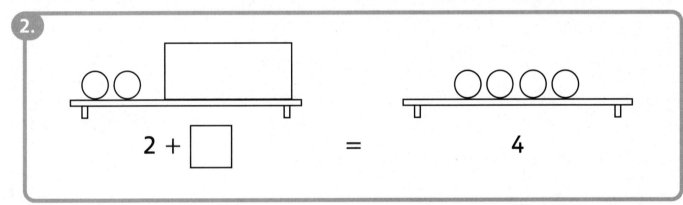

$$2 + \boxed{} \qquad = \qquad 4$$

3.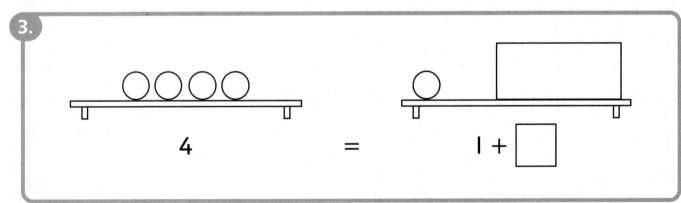

$$4 \qquad = \qquad 1 + \boxed{}$$

4.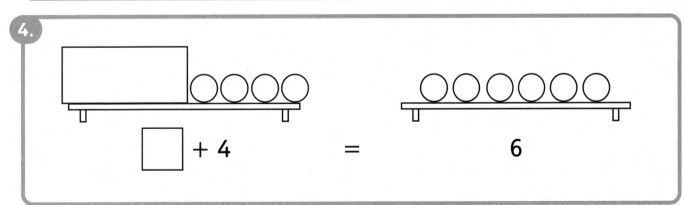

$$\boxed{} + 4 \qquad = \qquad 6$$

☐ Draw the hidden balls.

☐ Write the number of balls that are hidden.

5.

○○ + | ○○○ | = ○○○○○

2 + 3 = 5

6.

○○ + [   ] = ○○○

2 + ☐ = 3

7.

4 + [   ] = 6

4 + ☐ = 6

8.

2 + [   ] = 5

2 + ☐ = 5

9.

3 + [   ] = 6

3 + ☐ = 6

10.

3 + [   ] = 7

3 + ☐ = 7

11.

5 + [   ] = 8

5 + ☐ = 8

JUMP Math Accumula

59. Adding and How Many More

⬜ Draw 3 more circles.
⬜ Write the addition.

1.
3 more than 2

◉◉   ○○○

___2___ + ___3___

2.
3 more than 4

◉◉
◉◉

___4___ + _____

3.
3 more than 6

◉◉◉
◉◉◉

_____ + _____

4.
3 more than 3

◉◉
◉

_____ + _____

5.
3 more than 5

◉◉◉
◉◉

_____ + _____

6.
3 more than 1

◉

_____ + _____

7.
3 more than 7

◉◉◉◉
◉◉◉

_____ + _____

8.
3 more than 8

◉◉◉◉
◉◉◉◉

_____ + _____

☐ Draw more circles.
☐ Write the addition.

9.
2 more than 3

___3___ + ___2___

10.
1 more than 6

___6___ + _____

11.
3 more than 5

_____ + _____

12.
2 more than 7

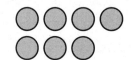

_____ + _____

13.
5 more than 4

_____ + _____

14.
3 more than 8

_____ + _____

15.
2 more than 6

_____ + _____

16.
4 more than 3

_____ + _____

☐ Draw more circles.
☐ Write the **addition sentence**.

17. 5 more than 2

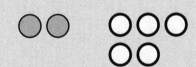

__2__ + __5__ = __7__

18. 2 more than 6

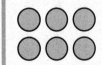

____ + ____ = ____

19. 4 more than 5

____ + ____ = ____

20. 6 more than 2

____ + ____ = ____

☐ Write an addition sentence to find the answer.

21. 3 more than 5

__5__ + __3__ = __8__

3 more than 5 is __8__.

22. 4 more than 6

____ + ____ = ____

4 more than 6 is ____.

23. 7 more than 10

____ + ____ = ____

7 more than 10 is ____.

24. 2 more than 16

____ + ____ = ____

2 more than 16 is ____.

60. Finding an Addend by Counting On

◻ Draw circles to find the missing number.

1.
$$3 + \boxed{2} = 5$$

2.
$$2 + \boxed{} = 6$$

3.
$$1 + \boxed{} = 5$$

4.
$$3 + \boxed{} = 6$$

5.
$$4 + \boxed{} = 7$$

6.
$$5 + \boxed{} = 6$$
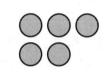

7.
$$\boxed{} + 2 = 5$$

8.
$$\boxed{} + 3 = 5$$

9.
$$\boxed{} + 2 = 4$$

10.
$$\boxed{} + 1 = 3$$

Raj **counts on** to find the missing number in the number sentence.

$$4 + \boxed{} = 6$$

1	2	3	4	5	6

4	5	6

He says "4" with his fist closed.
He counts up from 4 until he reaches 6.
The answer is the number of fingers up.

$$4 + \boxed{2} = 6$$

☐ Find the missing number by counting on.

11.
$$4 + \boxed{} = 7$$

12.
$$5 + \boxed{} = 6$$

13.
$$3 + \boxed{} = 5$$

14.
$$8 + \boxed{} = 10$$

15.
$$\boxed{} + 2 = 6$$

16.
$$\boxed{} + 3 = 4$$

17.
$$9 + \boxed{} = 14$$

18.
$$7 + \boxed{} = 12$$

19.
$$\boxed{} + 8 = 15$$

☐ Find the missing number by counting on.

20.
$5 + \boxed{} = 9$

21.
$6 + \boxed{} = 8$

22.
$6 + \boxed{} = 10$

23.
$8 + \boxed{} = 10$

24.
$\boxed{} + 2 = 6$

25.
$\boxed{} + 3 = 4$

26.
$\boxed{} + 16 = 19$

27.
$7 + \boxed{} = 12$

28.
$12 = 8 + \boxed{}$

29.
$15 = \boxed{} + 10$

30.
$\boxed{} + 14 = 19$

31.
$20 = \boxed{} + 17$

32. BONUS
$21 + \boxed{} = 23$

33. BONUS
$42 + \boxed{} = 46$

34. BONUS
$65 + \boxed{} = 68$

35. BONUS
$87 + \boxed{} = 90$

☐ Count on to find the missing number.
☐ Draw shaded and unshaded circles to check your answer.

36.
$3 + \boxed{} = 7$

37.
$4 + \boxed{} = 8$

38.
$9 = \boxed{} + 5$

61. Subtracting by Counting On

Find 5 − 2 by counting on from the smaller number.

1	2	3	4	5
⊗	⊗	○	○	○

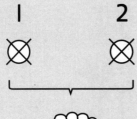 

2   3   4   5

The answer is the number of fingers you have up.

$$5 - 2 = 3$$

☐ Subtract by counting on from the smaller number.

1. 8 − 6 = ☐

2. 9 − 5 = ☐

3. 7 − 4 = ☐

4. 9 − 8 = ☐

5. 8 − 4 = ☐

6. 6 − 3 = ☐

7. 7 − 5 = ☐

8. 10 − 6 = ☐

9. 12 − 10 = ☐

10. 15 − 11 = ☐

11. 19 − 17 = ☐

12. 19 − 12 = ☐

Subtract by counting on.

13.
$11 - 8 = \boxed{}$

14.
$17 - 15 = \boxed{}$

15.
$13 - 10 = \boxed{}$

16.
$20 - 18 = \boxed{}$

17.
$\boxed{} = 9 - 4$

18.
$\boxed{} = 16 - 13$

19.
$\boxed{} = 19 - 14$

20.
$\boxed{} = 10 - 6$

21.
$20 - 16 = \boxed{}$

Count on to subtract.

22.
$11 - 6 = \boxed{}$

23.
$17 - 13 = \boxed{}$

24.
$\boxed{} = 13 - 8$

25.
$\boxed{} = 20 - 15$

26.
$19 - 16 = \boxed{}$

27.
$17 - 11 = \boxed{}$

28.
$20 - 13 = \boxed{}$

29.
$18 - 15 = \boxed{}$

30.
$18 - 10 = \boxed{}$

31.
$\boxed{} = 19 - 11$

32.
$\boxed{} = 20 - 11$

33.
$\boxed{} = 18 - 9$

☐ Subtract by counting on.

34.
$13 - 7 = \boxed{}$

35.
$\boxed{} = 18 - 14$

36.
$15 - 9 = \boxed{}$

37.
$\boxed{} = 16 - 8$

38.
$12 - 9 = \boxed{}$

39.
$\boxed{} = 16 - 14$

☐ Write the subtraction sentence to find the answer.

40.
Jill has 3 pears.
She eats 2 of them.
How many does she have left? ___*3 − 2 = 1*___

41.
Ava has 20 stamps.
She gives 17 to her friends.
How many does she have left? _____

42.
17 frogs are on a log. 13 hop off.
How many are still on the log? _____

43. BONUS
You have 12 marbles. You give some to your partner.
Now you have 8 marbles.
How many did you give away? _____

62. Number Sentences (3)

☐ Find the missing number by adding.

1.
$$3 + 5 = \boxed{8}$$

2.
$$6 + 2 = \boxed{}$$

3.
$$8 + 3 = \boxed{}$$

4.
$$\boxed{} = 5 + 4$$

5.
$$\boxed{} = 9 + 4$$

6.
$$6 + 6 = \boxed{}$$

☐ Find the missing number by counting on.

7.
$$2 + \boxed{7} = 9$$

8.
$$6 + \boxed{} = 8$$

9.
$$5 = 2 + \boxed{}$$

10.
$$9 + \boxed{} = 10$$

11.
$$18 = \boxed{} + 14$$

12.
$$2 + \boxed{} = 8$$

☐ Find the missing number by adding or counting on.

13.
$$5 + 4 = \boxed{}$$

14.
$$\boxed{} + 15 = 19$$

15.
$$2 + 14 = \boxed{}$$

16.
$$\boxed{} + 11 = 17$$

17.
$$12 + \boxed{} = 14$$

18.
$$18 + \boxed{} = 20$$

19.
$$16 + 1 = \boxed{}$$

20.
$$11 = \boxed{} + 7$$

21.
$$17 + 3 = \boxed{}$$

☐ Is the number sentence **true** or **false**?

22.
7 + 2 = 8

true   (false)

23.
10 + 2 = 12

true   false

24.
5 + 3 = 10

true   false

25.
8 + 3 = 11

true   false

26.
6 = 4 + 3

true   false

27.
17 = 3 + 14

true   false

28. BONUS
7 − 2 = 5

true   false

29. BONUS
9 − 4 = 6

true   false

☐ Write the answer.

30.
Jayden writes 3 + 7 = 10.
Is he correct? How do you know?

31.
8 rabbits are in a field.
6 hop away.

Write a number sentence to find
how many are left.

63. Identifying Parts and Totals

☐ What things are you adding?

1.

3 big frogs   2 small frogs

_____ *frogs* _____

2.

2 red marbles   4 green marbles

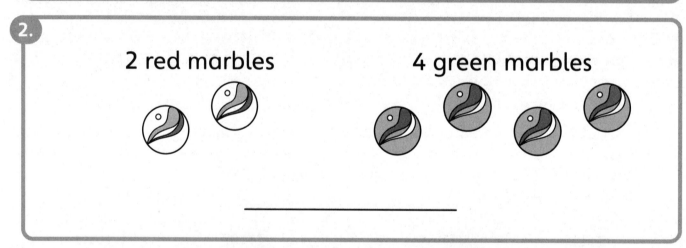

_____

3.

3 new pencils

5 used pencils

_____

4.

4 big keys

7 small keys

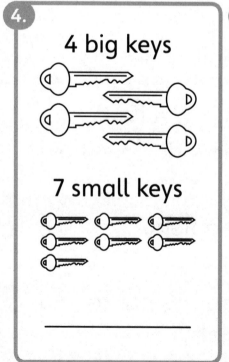

_____

5.

6 green apples

6 red apples

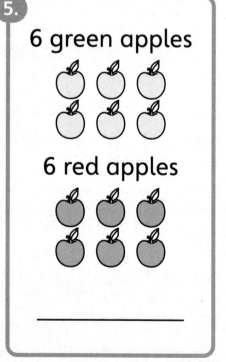

_____

☐ Add.

☐ Write what you are adding.

6.

There are 5 big frogs.

There are 2 small frogs.

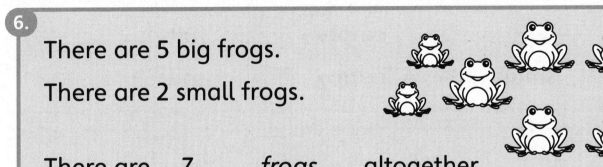

There are ___7___ ___frogs___ altogether.

7.

There are 4 new pencils.

There are 2 used pencils.

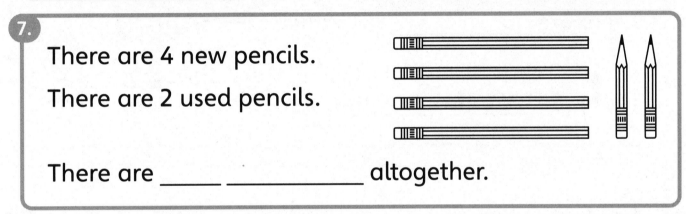

There are _____ _____ altogether.

8.

There are 5 green apples.

There are 5 red apples.

There are _____ _____ in total.

9.

There are 3 empty mugs.

There are 2 full mugs.

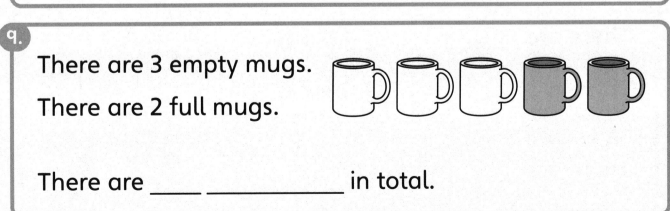

There are _____ _____ in total.

☐ Make a problem for the picture.
 Use words from the box.

~~big~~	empty	full
small	happy	sad

10.

There are __3__ __big__ frogs.

There are __2__ _____ frogs.

There are __5__ frogs altogether.

11.

There are ____ _____ bowls.

There are ____ _____ bowls.

There are __5__ bowls in total.

12.

There are ____ _____ faces.

There are ____ _____ faces.

There are ____ faces in total.

64. Drawing Pictures to Find Parts and Totals

There are 5 apples.

3 are red. The rest are green.

How many are green?

Draw 5 circles to
show 5 apples.

○○○○○

Shade 3 circles to
show 3 red apples.

●●●○○

There are 2 green apples.

There are red and green apples.

☐ Draw a picture to find how many are green.

1.
There are 4 apples.
3 are red.

●●●○

___/___ green apple

2.
There are 5 apples.
4 are red.

_____ green apple

3.
There are 3 apples.
I is red.

_____ green apples

4.
There are 6 apples.
2 are red.

_____ green apples

There are 3 red apples and 4 green apples.
How many apples are there in total?

Draw 3 red apples.

Draw 4 green apples.

There are 7 apples.

☐ Draw a picture to find the total number of apples.

5.
There are 2 red apples and 3 green apples.

___5___ apples

6.
There are 2 red apples and 2 green apples.

_____ apples

7.
There are 3 red apples.
There are 2 green apples.

_____ apples

8.
Jane has 2 red apples and I green apple.

_____ apples

9.
There are 4 red apples and 2 green apples in a bowl.

_____ apples

10.
Don has 3 green apples and I red apple.

_____ apples

□ Draw a picture to find the answer.

11.
Tony has 3 red apples and 3 green apples. How many apples does he have?

_____ apples

12.
Kate has 5 apples. 3 are red. The rest are green. How many are green?

_____ green apples

13.
3 red apples and 1 green apple fall out of a tree. How many apples fall?

_____ apples

14.
A bowl has 2 green apples and 3 red apples. How many apples are in the bowl?

_____ apples

15.
A bowl has 8 apples. 3 are green. The rest are red. How many are red?

_____ red apples

16.
A bowl has 5 red apples and 4 green apples. How many apples are in the bowl?

_____ apples

☐ Draw a picture to find the answer.

17.

Blanca has 3 yellow balls and 2 purple balls. How many balls does she have?

_____ balls

18.

Roy has 5 pets. 3 are fish. The rest are cats. How many cats does he have?

_____ cats

19. BONUS

Amy sees 12 birds. 7 are robins.
The rest are jays.
How many jays does she see?

_____ jays

20.

7 children are in a pool.
3 are girls. How many are boys?

21.

3 boys and 6 girls are in a pool.
How many children are in the pool?

65. Parts and Totals

☐ Draw circles for the apples.

1.
6 apples
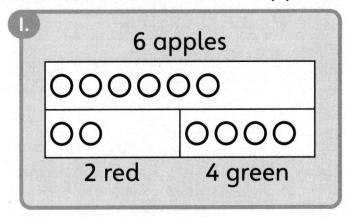
2 red — 4 green

2.
5 apples
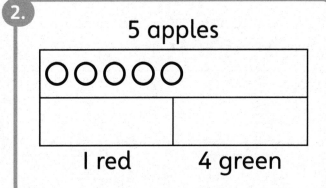
1 red — 4 green

3.
4 apples
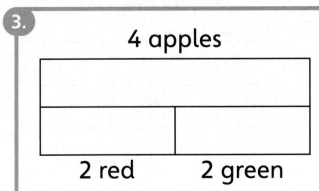
2 red — 2 green

4.
6 apples
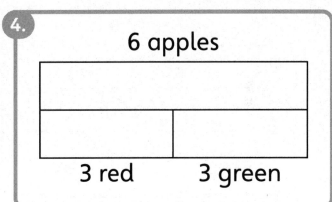
3 red — 3 green

5.
5 apples
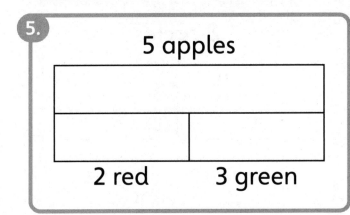
2 red — 3 green

6.
3 apples
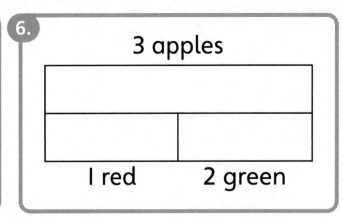
1 red — 2 green

7.
4 apples
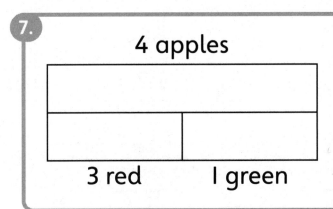
3 red — 1 green

8.
2 apples
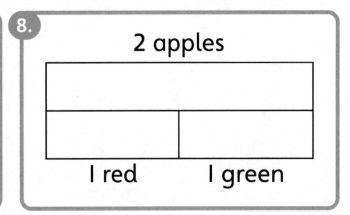
1 red — 1 green

☐ Draw circles to find the missing number.

9.

_____5_____ circles

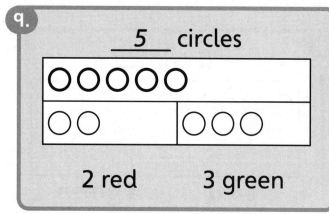

2 red   3 green

10.

5 circles

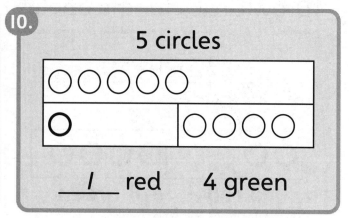

_____1_____ red   4 green

11.

_____ circles

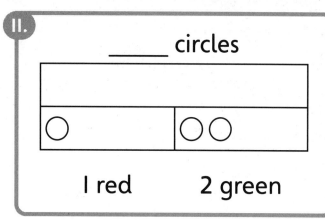

1 red   2 green

12.

_____ circles

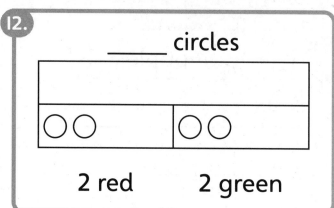

2 red   2 green

13.

4 circles

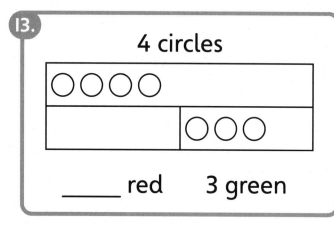

_____ red   3 green

14.

6 circles

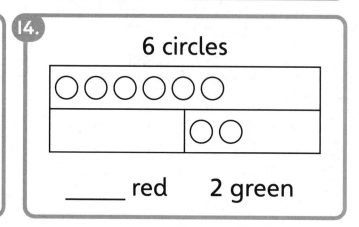

_____ red   2 green

15.

2 circles

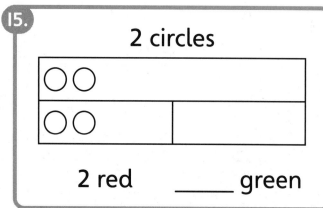

2 red   _____ green

16.

5 circles

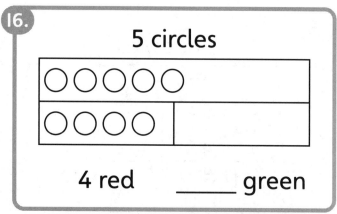

4 red   _____ green

☐ Find the missing number.

17.
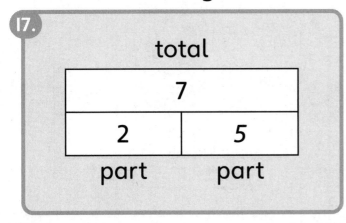

total	
7	
2	5
part	part

18.
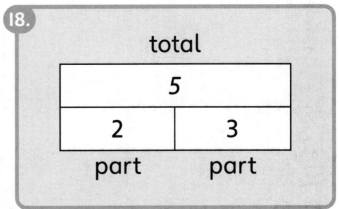

total	
5	
2	3
part	part

19.
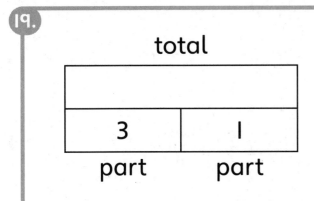

total	
3	1
part	part

20.
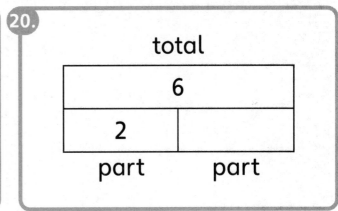

total	
6	
2	
part	part

21.
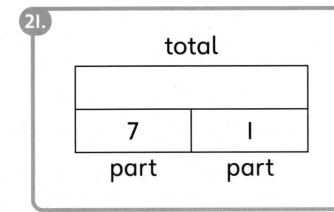

total	
7	1
part	part

22.
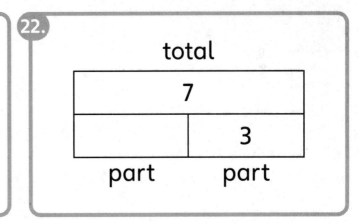

total	
7	
	3
part	part

23.
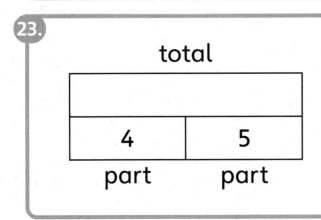

total	
4	5
part	part

24.
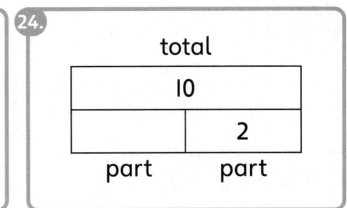

total	
10	
	2
part	part

☐ Find the missing number.

25.

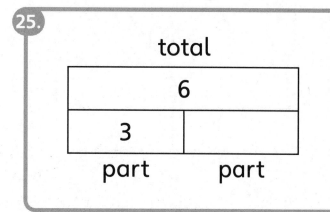

total

6	
3	
part	part

26.

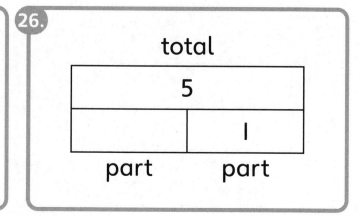

total

5	
	1
part	part

27.

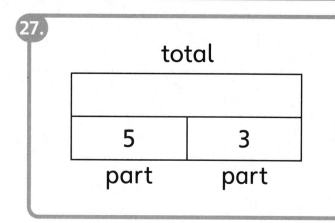

total

5	3
part	part

28.

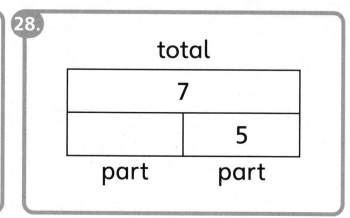

total

7	
	5
part	part

29.

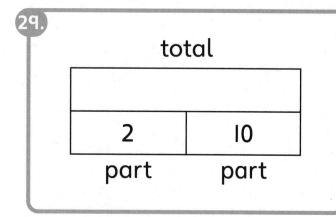

total

2	10
part	part

30.

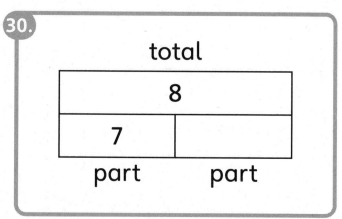

total

8	
7	
part	part

31. BONUS

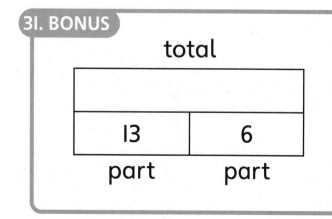

total

13	6
part	part

32. BONUS

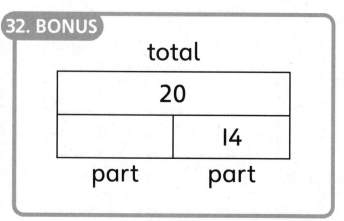

total

20	
	14
part	part

66. Parts, Totals, and Number Sentences

⬜ Write an addition sentence for the picture.

1.

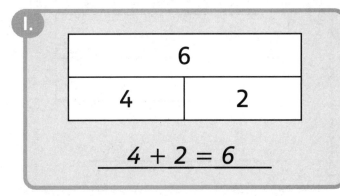

6	
4	2

___4 + 2 = 6___

2.

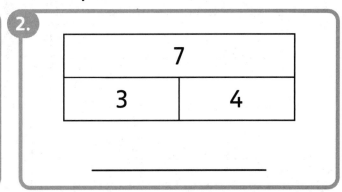

7	
3	4

_____

3.

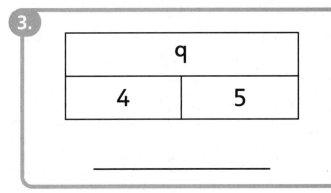

9	
4	5

_____

4.

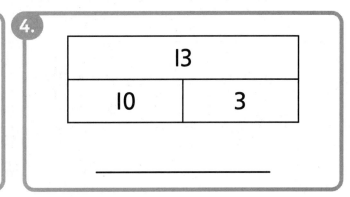

13	
10	3

_____

⬜ Write an addition sentence for the picture.
⬜ Draw ⬜ for the missing number.

5.

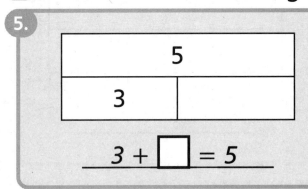

5	
3	

___3 + ⬜ = 5___

6.

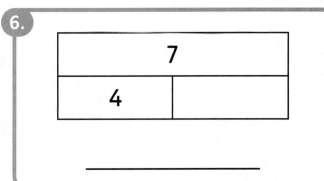

7	
4	

_____

7.

8	
5	

_____

8.

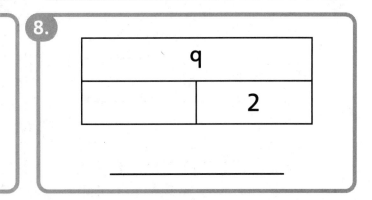

9	
	2

_____

☐ Write an addition sentence for the picture.

9.

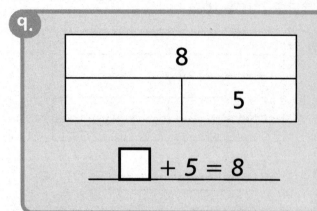

8	
	5

☐ + 5 = 8

_____

10.

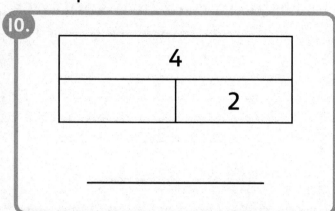

4	
	2

_____

11.

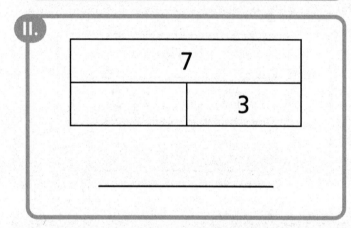

7	
	3

_____

12.

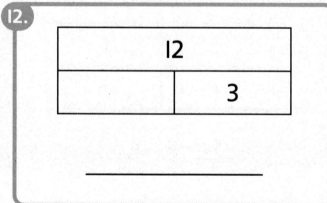

12	
	3

_____

13.

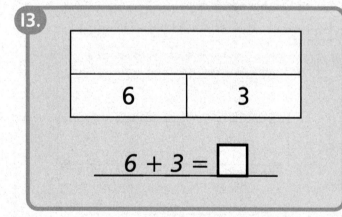

6	3

6 + 3 = ☐

_____

14.

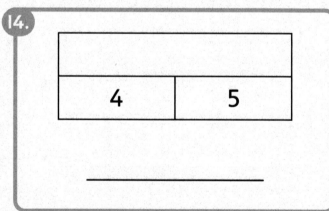

4	5

_____

15.

1	9

_____

16.

14	3

_____

☐ Fill in the missing numbers.

17.

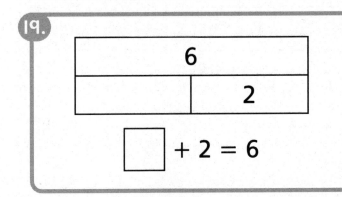

9	
2	7

$2 +$ ☐7☐ $= 9$

18.

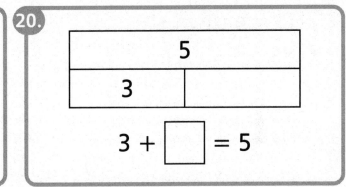

8	
3	5

$3 + 5 =$ ☐8☐

19.

6	
	2

☐ $+ 2 = 6$

20.

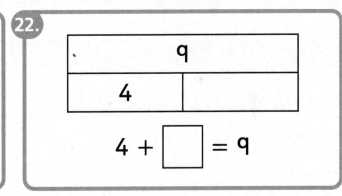

5	
3	

$3 +$ ☐ $= 5$

21.

2	8

$2 + 8 =$ ☐

22.

9	
4	

$4 +$ ☐ $= 9$

☐ Write a number sentence.
☐ Fill in the missing numbers.

23. BONUS

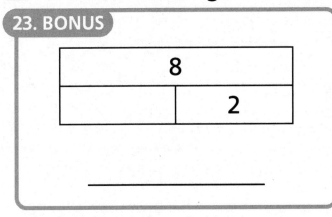

8	
	2

_____

24. BONUS

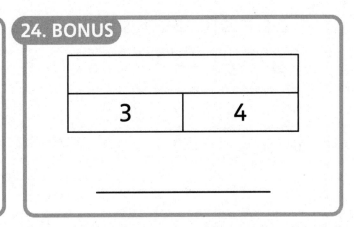

3	4

_____

67. Word Problems with Parts and Totals

☐ Write **?** for the missing number.
☐ Fill in the picture.

1.

Ken has 6 blue fish
and 5 green fish.

How many fish
does he have?

total

?	
6	5
part	part

2.

Lynn has 3 red pens
and 2 blue pens.

How many pens does
she have in all?

total

part	part

3.

There are 6 boys and
7 girls in a class.

How many students are
in the class?

total

part	part

☐ Write **?** for the missing number.
☐ Fill in the picture.

4.

Ivan has 5 crayons.
2 of them are red.
The rest are yellow.

How many are yellow?

total	
5	
2	?
part	part

5.

7 birds are on a branch.
3 of them are blue.
The rest are red.

How many are red?

total	
part	part

6.

14 students are on a bus.
9 of them are girls.

How many are boys?

total	
part	part

☐ Fill in the picture.
☐ Find the answer.

7.

Hanna has 3 red apples
and 4 green apples.
How many apples does she have?

___7___ apples

total	
7	
3	4
part	part

8.

Ravi has 8 animal stickers.
5 are lions. The rest are tigers.
How many tiger stickers does he have?

_____ tiger stickers

total	
part	part

9.

Grace finds pink shells and white shells.
She finds 8 shells. 6 are white.
How many are pink?

_____ pink shells

total	
part	part

10.

Jon has 12 fish and 2 dogs.
How many pets does he have?

_____ pets

total	
part	part

☐ Fill in the picture.
☐ Find the answer.

11.

Zara puts 5 dimes in her bank.
Then she puts in 6 dimes.
How many dimes does she put
in her bank altogether?

_____ dimes

total

part	part

12.

17 children play tag.
7 are boys.
How many are girls?

_____ girls

total

part	part

☐ Fill in the picture.
☐ Write the number sentence.
☐ Find the answer.

13. BONUS

7 girls and 9 boys play baseball.
How many children play baseball?

_____

_____ children play baseball

total

part	part